Before and After Violence

Margaret S. Mahler Series

This series of yearly volumes began appearing in 1991 and is based upon the panel discussions presented at the prestigious Annual Margaret Mahler Symposia held in Philadelphia. Each volume consists of three papers and their discussions presented at the most recent symposium. A thorough introduction and a comprehensive conclusion that pulls all the material together are specially written for the book. Occasionally, one or two papers that were not presented at the meeting but represent the cutting-edge thinking on the topic are also included. While this format and organization gives these books a friendly familiarity, the books' contents vary greatly and are invariably a source of excitement and clinical enthusiasm. Volumes published so far have addressed topics as diverse as hatred and cultural differences in childhood development, extramarital affairs and sibling relationship, mourning and self psychology, and resilience and boundary violations. Among the distinguished psychoanalysts whose work has appeared in this series are Salman Akhtar, Anni Bergman, Harold Blum, Ruth Fischer, Alvin Frank, Dorothy Holmes, Otto Kernberg, Selma Kramer, Peter Neubauer, Henri Parens, Fred Pine, John Munder Ross, and Ernest Wolf, to name a few. The vantage point is always broad-based and includes developmental, clinical, and cultural variables but the end point is consistently an enhancement of the technical armamentarium of the therapist.

Books Based Upon the Margaret S. Mahler Symposia

Thicker Than Blood: Bonds of Fantasy and Reality in Adoption (1999) by Salman Akhtar and Selma Kramer

Does God Help? Developmental and Clinical Aspects of Religious Belief (2000) edited by Salman Akhtar and Henri Parens

Three Faces of Mourning: Melancholia, Manic Defense, and Moving On (2001) edited by Salman Akhtar

Real and Imaginary Fathers: Development, Transference, and Healing (2004) edited by Salman Akhtar and Henri Parens

The Language of Emotions: Developmental, Psychopathology, and Technique (2005) edited by Salman Akhtar and Harold P. Blum

Interpersonal Boundaries: Variations and Violations (2006) edited by Salman Akhtar

Listening to Others: Developmental and Clinical Aspects of Empathy and Attunement (2007) edited by Salman Akhtar

The Unbroken Soul: Tragedy, Trauma, and Human Resilience (2008) edited by Henri Parens, Harold P. Blum, Salman Akhtar

Lying, Cheating, and Carrying On: Developmental, Clinical, and Sociocultural Aspects of Dishonesty and Deceit (2009) by Salman Akhtar and Henri Parens

The Electrified Mind: Development, Psychopathology, and Treatment in the Era of Cell Phones and the Internet (2011) edited by Salman Akhtar

The Mother and Her Child: Clinical Aspects of Attachment, Separation, and Loss (2012) edited by Salman Akhtar

Guilt: Origins, Manifestations, and Management (2013) edited by Salman Akhtar

Human Goodness: Origins, Manifestations, and Management (2014) edited by Salman Akhtar

The New Motherhoods: Patterns of Early Child Care in Contemporary Culture (2015) edited by Salman Akhtar

Divorce: Emotional Impact and Therapeutic Interventions (2016) edited by Salman Akhtar

Before and After Violence (2017) edited by Salman Akhtar

Before and After Violence

Developmental, Clinical, and Sociocultural Aspects

Edited by
Salman Akhtar

LEXINGTON BOOKS
Lanham • Boulder • New York • London

Published by Lexington Books
A wholly owned subsidiary of The Rowman & Littlefield Publishing Group, Inc.
4501 Forbes Boulevard, Suite 200, Lanham, Maryland 20706
www.rowman.com

Unit A, Whitacre Mews, 26-34 Stannary Street, London SE11 4AB

British Library Cataloguing in Publication Information Available

Library of Congress Cataloging-in-Publication Data Available

ISBN 978-1-4985-6858-6 (cloth: alk. paper)
ISBN 978-1-4985-6859-3 (electronic)

∞™ The paper used in this publication meets the minimum requirements of American National Standard for Information Sciences—Permanence of Paper for Printed Library Materials, ANSI/NISO Z39.48-1992.

Printed in the United States of America

To the memory of Margaret S. Mahler and Selma Kramer

Contents

Acknowledgments

All the chapters in this book, except chapters 1 and 8, were originally presented as papers at the 48th Annual Margaret S. Mahler Symposium on Child Development, held on April 15, 2017. We wish to express gratitude to the Department of Psychiatry of Jefferson Medical College, the main sponsor of this event. We are especially indebted to Dr. Michael Vergare, Chairman of the Department of Psychiatry and Human Behavior of the Jefferson Medical College, Mary Etezady, Chair of the Board of the Psychoanalytic Foundation of the Psychoanalytic Center of Philadelphia, and William Singletary, President of the Margaret S. Mahler Foundation for their continued kind support. There are many others who helped in subtle and not-so-subtle ways. To them, our most sincere thanks indeed. Finally, we wish to acknowledge deep appreciation of Ms. Jan Wright, for her superb organization of the symposium and for her skillful preparation of this book's manuscript.

Chapter 1

The Realm of Violence

An Overview

Salman Akhtar and Shawn Blue

Even though Sigmund Freud (1893) attributed it to an un-named English writer, he deserves the credit for popularizing the saying that "the man who first flung a word of abuse at his enemy instead of a spear was the founder of civilization" (p. 36). Regardless of its original source, the dictum does capture something of great beauty and meaning. The interpolation of thought and language between emotion and action is one of the cardinal achievements of humanity. Indeed, the common basis of human experience is constituted not only by a shared anatomy, physiognomy, and motivational substrate but also by a set of many other variables. These include "the capacity for thought and thinking, the acquisition of language, barriers against murder and incest, group affiliation, and the generative elaboration of myths and rituals" (Akhtar, 2003, pp. 131–132). The acquisition and sustenance of such "humanity," however, depends upon the individual's growing up and continuing to live in an "average expectable environment" (Hartmann, 1939) though constitutional givens also contribute to the achievement. An implication of this proposal is that if and when such hard-wired proclivities contain levels of anxiety and aggression that are difficult to "tame" and if and when the environment during formative years of childhood is unreliable, frustrating, and violating, then acquisition of "humanity" is tenuous and vulnerable to regression. Under such circumstances, thought becomes disordered, language regresses, prohibitions of murder and incest are weakened, and affect rapidly translates into action. Human propensity for violence, especially in its intense, cruel, and sustained form, is often the most devastating accompaniment of such malevolent transformation.

We select such violence as our focus in this contribution. Addressing both the origins and consequences of violence, we will divide our discourse in two major sections: "Antecedents, Settings, and Consequences," and "Remedies and Interventions." *In the first section,* we will tackle the occurrence of violence in (i) domestic, (ii) criminal, (iii) clinical, and (iv) political realms; in addition, we will address a category which, for the lack of a better term, can only be labelled (v) random violence. *In the second section,* we will delineate ameliorative strategies in (i) social, and (ii) clinical realms. We remain cognizant of potential overlaps in our categories just as we are aware that violence can be physical and mental as well as self-directed and other-directed. The schematic organization of our contribution is in the service of didactic clarity and by no means reflects oblivion to the concept of "over-determination" (Freud, 1895) and the "principle of multiple function" (Waelder, 1936).

ANTECEDENTS, SETTINGS, AND CONSEQUENCES

The setting in which violence takes place, the variables that propel its occurrence, and the results it leads to differ considerably. The accoutrements of brutality are myriad, the victims of many stripes, and the consequences range from transient humiliation through reactive fear and rage to life-long psychic damage. The following passages elucidate some of the scenarios involved in violence.

Domestic Violence

While we employ the commonplace expression, "domestic violence," we remain aware that it carries a certain heteronormative bias of prioritizing heterosexual relationships and marriage. McHugh and Frieze (2006) have especially highlighted how the terms "wife abuse" and "domestic violence" do not adequately or appropriately explain all situations in which violence occurs, such as in cases of same sex relationships and unmarried dating relationships. Although new terms have emerged to compensate for historical biases, (i.e., "dating violence" and "lesbian battering"), the term "intimate partner violence" is now increasingly used to address the violence that occurs in romantic relationships. Intimate partner violence includes psychological, physical, and sexual behaviors of a violent, stalking, and controlling nature. Perpetrators of such violence utilize domination, intimidation, and coercion (Dasgupta, 2002; Dutton and Goodman, 2005; Pence and Paymar, 1993) as well as isolation, surveillance, and jealousy. Often psychological and emotional abuse occurs before physical abuse. The emotionally abusive behaviors can involve constant criticism, intellectual and moral domination, and humiliation as well as manifold attempts to undermine one's confidence. Sexual coercion also constitutes a form of intimate partner violence. This can range from lascivious talk to forced sexual activities to refusal to use contraception and protection. Over time, the severity and frequency of violence increases within the relationship.

Stewart and Vigod (2017) utilized an ecological framework adapted by the World Health Organization (WHO) to classify risk factors for intimate partner violence into four areas: (i) *individual risk factors,* which include a history of child abuse, emotional disorders, violence, alcohol and substance use, limited education and intelligence, younger and older age, low income level, medical illness or physical disability, recent migration, sexual and ethnic minority and indigenous status; (ii) *relationship risk factors,* which include marital conflict, alcohol and substance use, exposure to parental violence, history of child abuse, poor parenting behaviors, low socioeconomic status, friendships with individuals who utilize violence, limited education, need for over-control, poor attitudes toward women, and constant need for additional sexual partners; (iii) *community risk factors*, which include poverty, high crime, unemployment, high mobility, lack of social cohesion, and inadequate ameliorative resources; (iv) *social risk factors*, which include the normalization of intimate partner violence (e.g., by joking about it), cultural acceptance of such violence, and the overall prevalence of gender inequality.

Stewart and Vigod (2017) acknowledge the multiple consequences of intimate partner violence on couples, families, social community, health system, and economy. Individuals experiencing violence in an intimate relationship are affected in both their physical and emotional health. Emotional effects include depression, anxiety, and posttraumatic stress disorder, as well as the vulnerability to develop risky behaviors (i.e., poor eating and sexual practices, alcohol, drug, and cigarette abuse). Other psychological consequences include emotional detachment, antisocial behavior, low self-esteem, difficulty trusting others, sleep disruption, self-harm, and suicidality (Stewart and Vigod, 2017; Zolotor, Denham and Weil, 2009). Physical effects of intimate partner violence include sexually transmitted diseases, brain, organ and dental injury, blindness/deafness, burns, lacerations and contusions, and death (Stewart and Vigod, 2017; Zolotor, Denham and Weil, 2009). Chronic conditions such as gastrointestinal disorders, cardiovascular disease, joint disease, bladder and kidney infections, migraines, headaches and asthma (Stewart and Vigod, 2017; Zolotor, Denham and Weil, 2009) can worsen. Infertility, miscarriage, and unintended pregnancies can also result (Stewart and Vigod, 2017; Zolotor, Denham and Weil, 2009). Pregnant women subject to violence often obtain prenatal care late or not at all, and often have premature babies or those with low-birth weight and vulnerability leading to perinatal death.

Unfortunately, many women tend to remain in chronically violent relationships due to economic concerns (Bowker, 1983; Browne and Williams, 1989), fear of disapproval from loved others (Dobash and Dobash, 1979; Frieze, 1979, Walker, 1979), learned helplessness (Walker, 1979; 1983;

1984), loss of identity (Chandler, 1986), emotional connection with abusing partner (Browne, 1987; Dutton and Painter, 1981; Walker, 1983), lack of access to helpful community resources (Gondolf and Fisher, 1988; Sullivan, Basta, Tan and Davidson, 1992), and fear of retaliation such as threats of being kidnapped or having children taken (Ridington, 1978; Stahly, 1996). This is evidenced by the fact that violence tends to escalate following a separation and divorce (Coker, Smith, McKeown and King, 2000) even resulting in death (Browne, 1987; Jones, 1981; Pagelow, 1981).

Same sex romantic relationships are no different in this regard (Greenwood, Relf, Huang, Pollack, Canchola and Cantania, 2002; Island and Letellier, 1991; Renzetti, 1989; 1992; Turell, 2000; Waldner-Haugrud, Gratch and Magruder, 1997). Influences such as power differential, victim-blaming, and the battered partner's hapless attempts to change the perpetrator's behavior (Brown, 2008; Elliott, 1996; Walsh, 1996) are also found in homosexual couples. Such couples can experience conflicts related to safe sex practices (Heintz and Melendez, 2006), their varying extents of internalized homophobia and transphobia (Greenwood et al., 2002), and the stress related to their being a minority (Balsam and Szymanski, 2005). An additional problem in the setting of violent homosexual couples is that the criminal justice system gets influenced by the perpetrator's sex and the couple's sexual orientation (Connolly, Huzurbazar and Routh-McGee, 2000; Island and Letellier, 1991; Letellier, 1996; Renzetti, 1989; Renzetti, 1992). Even the police are less likely to make arrests or enforce protection orders (Connolly et al., 2000; Renzetti, 1989) or intervene in situations of intimate partner violence (Renzetti, 1989). As a result, gay and lesbian couples who experience intimate partner violence might not receive the similar protection as heterosexual relationships. However, Seelau and Seelau (2005) found that gender and not sexual orientation determined how individuals witnessing an altercation would respond. Heterosexual relationships where males were the perpetrators were found to be more serious regarding threat of injury than heterosexual relationships with female perpetrators and gay and lesbian couples.

Child abuse often co-occurs in situations of intimate partner violence (Zolotor, Denham and Weil, 2009). Intimate partner violence also increases the potential of accidental injuries of children, either being held by parents during a violent altercation or when a child intercedes to end the altercation (Bair-Merritt, 2010). Children experiencing parental intimate partner violence often develop depression, anxiety, and posttraumatic stress disorder. They can also experience developmental delays and physical problems, including sleeping and eating disruption. Interpersonal problems including separation anxiety, aggressive behaviors, fearfulness, and hypervigilance can also occur and so do lowered self-esteem, school failure, substance abuse, and risky sexual practices. Such children attend less regular checkup visits and obtain less immunizations and are more likely to utilize emergency department services. Often their psychic lives are marred forever.

Criminal Violence

Here it is important to distinguish between affective violence and predatory violence (McEllistrem, 2004). Affective violence is defined by a presence of anger and fear and is the result of a perceived threat. It is often impulsive, reactionary, and emotional. Predatory violence lacks acute emotionality and perceived imminent threat. It is premeditated. A study of mass murderers and serial killers has accumulated several relevant characteristics (Melroy, Hempel, Gray, Mohandie, Shiva and Richards, 2004). A majority of adults and adolescents were portrayed as loners and tended to spend a great deal of time alone and not interacting with others. A good percentage of adults were preoccupied with weapons or war, had a history of violence (usually involving a female romantic partner), suffered from psychiatric illness (paranoid schizophrenia, delusional disorder, or major depression), or had severe personality disorders (narcissistic, antisocial, paranoid, and schizoid), often left threatening messages, were facing a triggering event, and had multiple weapons at their disposal.

Hate crimes refer to violence inflicted on individuals based on prejudicial beliefs on race, religion, sexual orientation, or ethnicity. Such violence does not only impact the individual but influences the individual's entire social status group, as well as society as a whole. Hate violence when compared to criminal violence includes an excessive level of destructiveness and multiple offenders (Downey and Stage, 1999), as well as increased psychological trauma (Sullaway, 2004). Studying the experience of hate violence, it appears that the occurrence of hate violence results in the victims' feeling powerless and mistrustful (Bard and Sangrey, 1986). Researching hate violence specifically in lesbian, gay, and bisexual individuals revealed greater psychological distress (Herek, Gillis and Cogan, 2000). As a result of hate violence, gay, lesbian, and bisexual individuals tended to perceive the world and people as unsafe and experienced feelings of powerlessness and vulnerability (Garnets, Herek and Levy, 1990). Levin and McDevitt (1995) and McDevitt, Levin and Bennett (2002) classified perpetrators of hate violence into four categories: (i) *thrill motivated offenders* who engage in violence to seek the right to brag and to be accepted by peers, (ii) *defensive offenders* who view other individuals different than themselves as a danger to their way of life, (iii) *mission offenders* who hold a supremacist belief system and, (iv) *retaliatory offenders* who have a desire to right a perceived wrong to their social group. Often the perpetrators of hate crimes show all four characteristics.

Although the majority of sexual violence occurs within intimate relationships, sexual violence and coercion can also occur with non-intimate partners. Verbal coercion used to obtain nonconsensual sex can include the utilization of blackmail, trickery, and threats. Sexual violence in the form of rape can be experienced when the individual is "ego-compromised" either through sleep, alcohol and/or drugs. Latane and Darley (1970) studied the patterns of how bystanders respond in times of emergencies and what motivates individuals to not intervene. As a result of their work, they created a five-step model of the process in which individuals intervene during a crisis as a bystander (Burn, 2009; Latane and Darley, 1970). The steps of this model include the individual noticing the event is occurring and then making the interpretation that an intervention is needed. The individual then makes a decision to take responsibility, makes a decision of how to help and finally takes some action to intervene in the situation.

Dating violence and sexual assault have both been identified as gender-based categories of violence. Compared to the typical experience of multiple occasions of violence that can occur in intimate partner violence, sexual assault usually occurs in a singular situation. In recent years, there has been study of sexual assault on college campuses due to the growing pattern of sexual violence that occurs in these settings. Also, the culture that exists on college campuses is argued to be influential in the prevalence of sexually violent behaviors. There is a body of research that identified college students hold belief of myths related to rape and hold biases related to individuals who experience sexual violence (Banyard, 2008; Burn, 2009; McMahon, 2010; Suarez and Gadalla, 2010). McMahon and Banyard (2012) offered Kelly's (1987) and Stout and McPhail's (1998) continuum of sexual violence as a model to explain the existence of the sexual culture on college campuses. This continuum utilizes feminist principles to describe the totality of sexually violent acts resulting from issues related to power and control. The continuum involves a range of acts that differ in levels of severity but all ultimately are connected in some way to each other (Kelly, 1987, 1989; Leidig, 1992; McMahon and Banyard, 2012; Osborne, 1995; Stout, 1991). Based on this continuum, sexual assault, rape, and criminally sexual behaviors would be defined as sexual violence (Stout and McPhail, 1998) and form the severest types of sexual violence with language, visual and media images, pornography, and harassment of a sexual nature falling on the other end of the spectrum. Whereas behaviors on the severe end of the spectrum are understood as criminal with associated enforceable laws and legal guidelines if they are perpetrated, behaviors on the other end of the continuum are seen as common and are not readily perceived of as negative and as damaging (McMahon and Banyard, 2012; Stout, 1991). However, these behaviors are seen to add to the systematic process of violence toward woman (Brownmiller, 1975; McMahon and Banyard, 2012; Sanday, 2007; Schwartz and Dekeseredy, 1997) which create a *rape supportive culture* (Buchwald, 1993; McMahon and Banyard, 2012; Sanday, 1981). All of the behaviors and acts on the continuum are viewed as some form of sexual violence and as detrimental to the healthy respect of women. The utility of bystander interventions is seen in the opportunity it allows for utilization at various points on the continuum. In addition, it provides a set of interventions that can be directed at the multiple sexually violent behaviors along the continuum (McMahon and Banyard, 2012).

Studying the effect of sexual violence on military women during their terms of service, it was found that these women reported poor health status when compared to military women who hadn't experienced sexual violence (Sadler, Booth, Nielson and Doebbeling, 2000). In fact, the emotional and physical effects of experiencing sexual violence evolved into similar health profiles of individuals diagnosed with major chronic illnesses. Results also showed differences related to physical and sexual violence. Those who experienced physical violence endorsed concerns related to their physical health status; however, those who reported experiencing sexual violence described both poor physical and emotional health as well as educational and economic deficits. Sadler et al. (2000) suggested that the finding of the chronicity and severity of health status as a result of physical and sexual violence could be due to the repeated exposure to violence during military service. These researchers also noted that obstetrician-gynecologists could be valuable resources to recognize the medical outcomes of sexual and physical violence of women.

Political Violence

Political praxis in democratic societies rests upon translating a value-driven social vision into enforceable governmental policies. This is accomplished by garnering public support for the cause, convincing the electorate, and negotiating with the members of the elected opposition. With rare exceptions, the process and discourse skirts breakthrough of primitive affects. Under different circumstances, the scenario turns more emotionally charged, cognitively biased, and replete with vituperative exchanges. This tends to happen when the democracy is being mocked by those in authority, when the democracy is a façade for theocracy, or when the government turns into a puppet for autocratic and dictatorial elected representatives. Worse developments occur when two nations are in conflict or when the very definition of a nation is perverted by the exclusive domination of one of its groups over the over. All sorts of conflicts then arise which can range from popular uprisings, freedom movements, terrorism, and civil war. And, here begins a huge linguistic, conceptual, and political conundrum. Take a look at the following four points.

- *First*, even though jettisoned in popular discourse, the word "terrorism" originated in connection with state-sponsored suppression of dissent. The word entered the English lexicon in 1795, when it referred to the governmental suppression of defiance by pumping fear in the arteries of its subjects. The term was derived from the French Revolutionary statesman Maximilien de Robespierre's Reign of Terror (1785–1794). From then on, the world has witnessed many horrific examples of such "terrorism from above," including the purges of Joseph Stalin (1878–1953), the Holocaust of Adolf Hitler (1889–1945), the killing fields of the regime of Pol Pot (1925–1993), and the torture chambers of August Pinochét (1915–2006). Arguably, the illegitimate and brutal invasion of Iraq by George W. Bush (1946–present) can also form an example of "terrorism from above." On a lesser scale, the assassination of nearly 30,000 Haitians by François Duvalier (1907–1971), the ruthless persecution of ethnic minorities in Uganda by Idi Amin (1925–2003), and the stunning atrocities by Hissène Habrè (1942–present) in Chad during the 1980s can also qualify as "terrorism from above." Yet, both the professional and popular coverage of terrorism gives far more attention to the "terrorism from below," that is, the mayhem let loose by comparably small groups of people who, for real or imaginary reasons, consider themselves humiliated and disenfranchised. Another point to remember is that "terrorism from below" is the weapon of the weaker party in the conflict; it has two choices: either surrender and accept defeat or to devise home-made means to fight one's enemy. The decision to take the latter route is less ideological and more tactical—maximum benefits to be accrued from minimum resources.
- *Second*, the designation "terrorist" is not a self-earned medal of identity. It is assigned to one by others who might be driven by politico-economic expedience and narrow self-interests. Thus, the British, at different eras in their history, have regarded George Washington (1732–1799), Subhash Chandra Bose (1897–1945), and Menachem Begin (1913–1992) as terrorists, while the respective American, Indian, and Israeli followers of these leaders upheld them to be great freedom-fighters. Moreover, someone labelled "terrorist" one day can be celebrated as an "outstanding contributor to world peace" the next day. In 1987, the United States held that Nelson Mandela's (1918–2013) African National Congress was one of the world's "most notorious terrorist groups" (Chomsky, 2003, p. 190), but six years later celebrated his receiving the Nobel Peace Prize. The leader of the Palestine Liberation Organization, Yasser Arafat (1929–2004), was long held to be a terrorist by the United States and Israel but later in his political career was awarded the 1994 Nobel Prize for Peace. More recently, Narendra Modi (1950–present), leader of the right-wing Hindu fundamentalist BJP (Bhartiya Janata Party), was barred entry into the United States for

being a terrorist. Upon becoming India's prime minister, however, Modi was not only allowed travel to the United States, but was feted with great fanfare by President Barack Obama in June 2016. Who is and who is not a terrorist (and what is and what is not a terrorist act) thus comes to lie in the proverbial eye of the beholder, and how clear and far-sighted is such eye's vision is not easy to tell.

- *Third,* while most "terrorist attacks" of today are traceable to Muslim groups of this or that stripe, the politico-religious violence subsumed under the label of "terrorism" is not exclusive to any religion. One does not have to invoke the Crusades (the intermittent religious military campaigns from 1096–1291), which Pope Urban II declared to be the will of God, in order to illustrate this point. The warring Protestants and Catholics of Ireland, the Tamil Tigers of Sri Lanka, the Khalistan secessionists and Maoist Naxalites of India, and the Basque separatists of Spain give testimony to the deployment of terrorist tactics by Christian, Hindus, and Sikhs alike. And, as none other than the Israeli prime minister Benjamin Netanyahu (1949-present) has acknowledged, "there are also acts of terror committed by Jews" (cited in *Israelam*, December 23, 2015). Moreover, history tells us that the practice of suicidal terrorism—reflexively equated with today's Muslims—goes quite far back and elements of it can be found in the tactics of the 1st-century Jewish Zealots and Sicarri, the 11th-century Ismaili Assassins of Northern Iran, and the 20th-century Japanese Kamikazes. Such practices were given the contemporary form of suicide bombing by the Tamil Tigers, a Marxist-Leninist Hindu group of Sri Lanka, and only later adopted by Muslim terrorists of the Middle East. In fact, the prime minister of India, Rajiv Gandhi (1944–1991), was killed by a Hindu woman suicide bomber of this group.
- *Fourth*, the gamut of violence subsumed under "terrorism" varies greatly. It ranges from the savagery of lone actors (e.g., Timothy McVeigh of Oklahoma City bombing; Nidal Hasan, who killed thirteen and injured thirty people at the Fort Hood, Texas, military base; Baruch Goldstein who, in 1994, showered bullets on Muslim Palestinians praying in a mosque, killing twenty-nine worshippers and wounding another 125; and Dylann Roof, the white supremacist who recently killed nine African American people in a mass shooting at a South Carolina Bible study), through the nefarious rampage of gangs (e.g., Beider-Meinhoff in Germany) to the mass violence caused by the political right (e.g., Ku Klux Klan in the United States of the 1950s) or the political left (e.g., the Shining Path Guerillas of Peru, the Naxalites of India) or by religious zealots (e.g., Boko Haram of Nigeria). Thus, all "terrorist attacks" are not the same. There are different kinds, different degrees, different motivations, and different results involved here.

The ground becomes more murky when we try to distinguish "terrorism" from "war." The tongue-in-cheek quip that a cult is a small religion and a religion is a big cult comes to our aid here. Terrorism is weak and poor peoples' war and war is powerful and rich peoples' terrorism. The former justify their aggression by pointing to their being oppressed. The latter regard theirs as necessary self-protection; they label their actions as "counterterrorism." The powerful blame the weak for brutalizing civilians while ignoring their own massacre of innocents; their victims are invariably "insurgents" and "militants." What gets overlooked in all this mayhem is that few wars are "justified wars" (e.g., protecting innocents, right intentions, last resort; see Elshtain, 2002) and that "war against terrorism" only begets "terrorism against war." The cycle of violence thus repeats.

Of course, one cannot end this discussion of politically motivated terrorism without mentioning the assassination of great leaders. In the United States alone, such brutality includes the murder of Abraham Lincoln (1865), John F. Kennedy (1963), Malcolm X (1965), Martin Luther King, Jr. (1968), and Robert Kennedy (1968). But, the pattern extends to other geopolitical locales as well. India, Bangladesh, Egypt, Israel, Egypt, and Pakistan have witnessed the politically motivated murders of Gandhi (1948), Sheikh Mujib-ur-Rahman (1975), Anwar el-Sadat (1981), Yitzhak Rabin (1995), and Benazir Bhutto (2007), respectively. In most such circumstances, an intricate blend of ontogenetically determined rage, actual or imagined threats to one's group identity, and autohypnosis with political overtones drive the violent action. The attempted killing of Ronald Regan (1981) was, however, an exception and had surprisingly little actual or imaginary basis: it was related to the malignant erotomania of a single individual.

Clinical Violence

Psychiatrists and emergency medicine physicians have a higher risk of experiencing violence and nurses, pharmacists, therapists and social workers also have a high risk of experiencing violence, with nursing staff having the greatest risk (Morrison, Lantos and Levinson, 1998). Front desk staff and receptionists in psychiatric clinics also have a greater risk of experiencing violence (Privitera, Weisman, Cerulli and Groman, 2005). Several factors also have been associated with a higher chance of patient violence (Madden, Lion and Penna, 1976; Foust and Rhee, 1993; Dubin, 1981), including physician inexperience, urban location, intoxication, and emotional conditions such as psychosis, delirium, schizophrenia, and alcohol and drug use (Madden, Lion and Penna, 1976; Foust and Rhee, 1993; Dubin, 1981; Iozzino, Ferrari, Large, Nielssen and de Girolamo, 2015; Madden and Lion, 1976). In outpatient settings, borderline, antisocial, and paranoid patients are more prone to violent acting-out.

It appears that experiencing the consequences of violence by patients is similar to experiencing a crime or a natural disaster (Erdos and Hughes, 2001). Although it appears that the majority of cases of violence include verbal threats and injuries, there are a significant number of situations that result in workplace deaths. Health professionals who experience violence have associated symptoms of fear, anxiety, anger, self-blame, and issues related to confidence (Lanza, 1996; Morrison, Lantos and Levinson, 1998), as well as posttraumatic stress disorder, guilt and shame (Nolan, Dallender, Soares, Thomsen and Arnetz, 1996). Many individuals experience symptoms of posttraumatic stress disorder, especially startle response, sleep disruptions, bodily tension, and soreness (Erdos and Hughes, 2001). Experiencing violence can cause considerable conflict for mental health professionals: they have a desire to help others but do not want to be physically injured in the process. In addition, health-care professionals tend to underreport the occurrence of violence due to the experience of shame (Harris, 1989), the perception that the occurrence is an isolated situation or they believe they have some responsibility in the violent occurrence (Morrison, Lantos and Levinson, 1998) or that it is part of their job (Harris, 1989). Violent situations are often experienced in psychiatry residency settings (Fink, Shroyer and Dubin, 1991; Madden, Lion and Penna, 1976; Rueve and Welton, 2008; Whitman, Armao and Dent, 1976), with the highest occurrence in emergency departments, prisons, and state hospital forensic units (Madden et al., 1976).

Morrison et al. (1998) suggest that violence is initiated by patients for several reasons. Patients might utilize violence as a means of communication during situations of conflict. In addition, patients might have dissatisfaction with their medical or psychiatric care or treatment progress. Furthermore, patients might perceive physicians as being similar to parents and will have unconditional acceptance of inappropriate behaviors. Patients might utilize violence as a mechanism to control situations of perceived powerlessness of medical crises. Finally, patients describe experiencing trauma when being secluded, restrained, and medicated against their will and engage in reactive violence (Olofsson and Jacobsson, 2001; Daffern, Mayer and Martin, 2006).

Violence also occurs with nonpatients, including family members, caretakers, and acquaintances (Morrison et al., 1998). In addition, other incidents of violence are associated with former employees, supervisors, in situations of theft and personal or domestic disputes (Bachman, 1996; Feldmann, Holt and Hellard, 1997; Morrison et al., 1998).

There are a number of costs related to violence in the health-care system. Medical costs due to time away from work and counseling services lead to financial loss incurred by the health-care institution (Campbell et al., 2011;

Morrison, Lantos and Levinson, 1998). Mental health staff and employees experience a decrease in job satisfaction as well as a desire to leave or resign from the organization (Sofield and Salmond, 2003). Other outcomes of violence in the workplace include staff turnover (Owen, Tarantello and Jones, 1998), time away from work, medical errors, injury claims (Ito, Eisen, Sederer, Yamada and Tachimoro, 2001; Roche, Diers, Duffield and Catling-Paull, 2009), and lowered quality of patient care (Campbell et al., 2011).

Random Violence

That a category of "random violence" forced itself upon our didactic stream of thought is itself a sad commentary on the state of affairs in our nation. We say this because while occasional outbursts of such violence might occur elsewhere, the phenomenon of "random violence" seems quintessentially American. The instances we have in mind for this group of violent acts share the following characteristics: (i) it is entirely unexpected, (ii) the victims are totally innocent, (iii) it is not restricted to crime-ridden areas but can pop up in utterly serene and bucolic settings, and (iv) its perpetrator has no personal or political axe to grind. The following five incidences illustrate such violence, though more examples can be readily given:

- *The April 20, 1999, Columbine massacre*: Seventeen-year-old Dylan Klebold and eighteen-year-old Eric Harris shot and killed thirteen people and wounded twenty-three others before killing themselves at Columbine High School, outside of Littleton, Colorado. The tragedy is among the worst mass shootings in US history.
- *The 2002, Washington DC area sniper killings*: The perpetrators—seventeen-year-old Lee Boyd Malvo and the much older John Allen Mohammad—acted from long distance and had little emotional involvement with their victims. In avoiding "intimacy" with their victims, they differed from ordinary serial killers. In lacking political motivation, they differed from terrorists. Theirs was a strange case which nonetheless brought enormous terror to the region where they operated.
- *The July 20, 2002, mass killing in the theater*: Twenty-year-old James Holmes shot and killed twelve people and injured seventy others in a theater at a midnight show in Aurora, Colorado. He had rigged his apartment with explosives; however, he was caught. He pleaded "not guilty by reason of insanity." He was convicted of twenty-four counts of first-degree murder, 140 counts of attempted first-degree murder, and one count of possessing explosives in July 2015. In August 2015, he was sentenced to life in prison without the possibility of parole: he was given twelve life sentences

(one for every person he killed), and 3,318 years for the attempted murders of those he wounded and for rigging his apartment with explosives.
- *The December 14, 2012, Sandy Hook massacre*: Twenty-year-old Adam Lanza fatally shot twenty elementary-school-aged children, six to seven years old, and six other school staff members at Sandy Hook Elementary School in Newtown, Connecticut. He had shot and killed his mother at home prior to coming to the school. He killed himself after the massacre. The tragedy is the deadliest mass shooting at either an elementary or high school, and the third deadliest shooting by a lone person in the United States.
- *The June 28, 2017, road rage killing*: Twenty-eight-year-old David Desper shot and killed eighteen-year-old Bianca Roberson while they both were attempting to merge into the same lane on Route 100 in Chester County in Pennsylvania. He shot her in the left side of her head while they were both driving. She was killed immediately and crashed her car into car into a ditch. He hid out for a few days then turned himself in.

As stated above, such mayhem happens unexpectedly, often in serene settings, and is directed at hapless and unsuspecting civilians, including children. "Random violence" is thus distinct from domestic violence which occurs in intimate relationships, political violence which arises from socio-cultural grudges, clinical violence which emanates from psychopathology, and criminal violence which arises from disturbances of conscience and an admixture of need and greed. Just as these five kinds of violence have overlaps and distinctions, so do the ameliorative strategies to curtail this regrettable form of human behavior.

REMEDIES AND INTERVENTIONS

We will divide our comments on the multifaceted strategies to reduce violence into (i) community-based interventions, and (ii) clinical interventions. We do not take the manic route to thinking that all violence can be eliminated; the instinctual and socioeconomic vectors driving it are too deeply entrenched to be susceptible to complete elimination. Reduction, in fact considerable reduction, is, we believe, possible and that's what our proposals aim to achieve.

Community-Based Interventions

Major issues to consider in social strategies for amelioration of violence include targeting themes of power, control, and gender roles as well as governmental policies toward gun control. Preventive measures need to be created, such as educational programs defining these issues and how they impact not only intimate relationships, but also relationships in general. Support, education, and counseling in the form of parenting behaviors and intimate interactions will also improve the relationship dynamics of romantic relationships and families. Since alcohol and drug use plays a major role in violent behavior, the provision of healthy and effective coping strategies as well as rehabilitation and treatment of alcohol/drug abuse will be important in addressing the influence of alcohol and drugs in the practice of violence. As recommended before, better screening and assessment of violence should be employed in all settings. Another issue that must be considered involves the pattern of silence that is pervasive in the culture of violence. Most likely due to the result of society's acceptance of violent behaviors, much of the existence of violence is hidden by a culture of silence. As society begins to take a clearer stand against the perpetuation of violence, the closer it will get to ending its occurrence. The culture of violence that exists within the military and during war was also investigated. Further acknowledgment needs to emphasize the traumatization and added violence that occurs within individuals in the military. Finally, issues related to sexism need to be acknowledged when describing the prevalence of violence. Acknowledging that violence also exists within same sex romantic relationships and with trans individuals is extremely important in addressing the violence that is experienced by all members of society.

Gun control continues to be a controversial topic in today's society. Yet due to the violence of mass shootings, murder, and injury that pervades society, gun control must be addressed in order to ensure a safer society. Not only does uncontrolled gun possession lead to death and injury, it also creates a culture of fear as well as grief. In addition, it disrupts one's sense of safety and stability especially in settings where safety is often perceived to be inherent (i.e., home, neighborhood, academic and religious institutions). It is imperative that gun control is taken more seriously in order to begin the end to violence that occurs within society. Rigidly clinging to the 2nd Amendment provision can cloak hostile intentions under the noble garment of patriotism. This needs re-visiting and revision.

Racism and sexism continue to plague society. The violence that occurs as a result of hate crimes illustrates the depth of prejudicial beliefs on behavior. Again, a continuum of severe behaviors as well as those behaviors that are less severe but also damaging applies to the process of racism and sexism that exists. In addition, societal acceptance of these behaviors or lack of intervention when these behaviors are witnessed only further perpetuates the existence of racism and sexism and also allows the expression of violence against individuals seen as different than mainstream society. Hate speech has become normalized in today's world and therefore, its consequences are often overlooked. Allowing hate speech to exist provides permission for violence against whom one holds prejudicial beliefs.

Finally, by addressing the sexually ill-informed, biased, and misogynistic "norms," sexual violence on college campuses and in society at large can be controlled (Kelly, 1987; Stout and McPhail, 1998). Abolishing a rape or sexually violent supportive culture will begin to break down the factors that lead to sexual violence. In addition, bystander programs and interventions will encourage the greater society to intervene and explicitly acknowledge that sexual violence is inappropriate and detrimental. It is argued that this continuum model can also be applied to the case of intimate partner physical, sexual, and emotional violence. Within intimate partner violence there are a range of behaviors that constitute the violence that occurs within these relationships. Similar to the continuum of sexual violence, this proposed continuum would also involve behaviors that differ in severity but again are all connected to each other. Also, similar to the sexual violence continuum, this one would include the most severe forms of violence on one end of the spectrum (i.e., those punishable by law) with damaging forms of violence on the other end (i.e., jokes, comments, etc.). When these behaviors are seen as a systematic process, it becomes clear about the depth of change that needs to occur to demolish this pattern of behaviors.

Clinical Interventions

Keeping in mind that our readership is mainly psychotherapists and psychoanalysts, we will focus on the management of rage, hate, and potential violence in outpatient clinical practices. We are aware that a considerable literature exists about the treatment of such tendencies (especially when associated with psychotic regression) in inpatient settings, and that this literature addresses the modalities of psychopharmacology, milieu therapy, behavior modification, and the use of seclusion and restraints. Both hospitalized patients and their caretakers need attention if one has to reduce the possibility of violent outbursts: (i) *patients* could be provided psychoeducation including verbal communication, conflict resolution, affect regulation, use of assertive behaviors, self-awareness of anger, and the ways to remove oneself from the triggering situation (Sheridan, Henrion, Robinson and Baxter, 1990). Anderson and West (2011) suggested that in the risk assessment of potentially violent patients one must consider the patient's awareness of the illness, the nature of the violence (i.e., result of psychosis), medication compliance, access to weapons, the level of structure and available support system in the patient's life (Anderson and West, 2011); (ii) *physicians* and other caretakers must pay attention to signs from patients that make them experience fear of feel threatened (Morrison et al., 1998; Rice and Moore, 1991). Precautions that physicians can consider include maintenance of physical space between the office door and the violent person, keeping a violent person within sight, and the removal of items that could be utilized as weapons (Dubin, 1981; Morrison et al., 1998; Rice and Moore, 1991). Morrison et al. (1998) offer several interventions to consider when creating a violence prevention program. Health-care administration must commit to initiating a program that addresses violence through training, crisis management, debriefing, and surveillance programs. Training and education should be provided to all employees, including managers, supervisors, and security staff. Psychiatric residency programs should provide education and training regarding the assessment and management of violence (Antonius, Fuchs, Herbert et al., 2010) as well as self-protection (Anderson and West, 2011). Anderson and West (2011) also suggested that the administration of health-care settings should encourage the reporting of violent occurrences and provide support to employees who do report incidents. All this pertains to the inpatient setting.

In outpatient management of hateful and destructive tendencies, we take Kernberg's (1995) important work in this realm as our starting point. Approaching specific technical interventions to the treatment of individuals with intense hatred and potential for violence, he makes the following seven suggestions: (i) assess the realistic risks of unleashing destructive forces from within the patient and the possibility of their being contained by the patient's ego and the therapeutic frame; (ii) judiciously use various auxiliary measures, including a firm initial contract to structure the treatment in order to minimize risks to the patient, therapist, and others; (iii) diagnose secondary defenses against hatred and consistently interpret them, with full awareness that such interventions might shift a quiet psychopathic transference (involving deceptiveness, dishonesty, and deliberate withholding of information) to a more heated paranoid one; (iv) help the patient become aware of his pleasure in hatred, thus seeking to render it ego-syntonic; (v) interpret the patient's paranoid reaction including acknowledge the incompatible views of "reality" help by the patient and the therapist; (vi) identify, circumscribe, and tolerate such a "psychotic nucleus" in the transference before attempting to resolve it interpretively; and, (vii) interpret, in relatively traditional manner, the guilt-ridden depressive transferences that emerge after the resolution of paranoid transferences.

While emphasizing the necessity to discern defenses *against* hatred, Kernberg does not pay adequate attention to the alternate formulation, that is, the defensive functions *of* hatred (e.g., against dependent longings in the transference). The issue, we must emphasize, is not whether hatred in transference is an activation of an early victim-victimizer relationship (however distorted by fantasy) or is itself a defense against "the dread to resourceless dependence" (Khan, 1972). It is not an either/or situation since "in the flow and flux of analytic material we are always in the world of 'both'/and'" (Wallerstein, 1983, p. 31).

Three other points need to be considered as one works with hateful and potentially violent patients. *First*, the function of "holding" (Winnicott, 1960; Lewin and Schulz, 1992) often plays a greater role in interpretive unmasking and reconstruction. *Second*, the patient's overt hatred and destructive fantasies (and acts) might be the manifestation of his unconscious hope that the analyst will survive such attacks and, in doing so, detoxify his relentless need for revenge. *Third*, a patient in the throes of intense hatred does not actually have a reasonable portion of his ego allied with the analyst. The patient is neither able nor receptive to the interpretive undertaking. "When deeply regressed, the patient cannot identify with the analyst or appreciate his point of view any more than the fetus or newly born can sympathize with the mother" (Winnicott, 1947, p. 202).

This brings up the clinical situation of "emotional flooding" (Volkan, 1976), whereby the patient gets so enraged during a clinical session that he seems to explode and become violent. According to Volkan, the first manifestation of such "flooding" is

> usually an accumulation of memories and fantasies (flooding in the ideational field) that support the same emotion. The patient can refer to these memories or fantasies only in a kind of "shorthand"—fragmentary sentences, or a single world. He may then begin stuttering and lose the power of intelligible speech altogether. It is impossible at this point to distinguish between flooding in the emotional, actional, or ideational field. The patient may scream and exhibit diffuse motor activity; he may seem to have lost his human identity . . . . Patients capable of reporting their experience of emotional flooding after the even usually indicate that strange perceptual changes took place. They underwent a "metamorphosis" during the experience, becoming monstrous and diabolical when signal affects were replaced by primal affects closely related to the aggressive drive (pp. 179, 183).

Such emotional outbursts are of little psychotherapeutic use. During them, the patient does not seem amenable to interpretive interventions; not enough observing ego is available to him. Their usefulness lies in their detoxifying effects over a long period of therapy and in their providing foci for proper, in-depth investigation during calmer times. While they are occurring, the therapist must avoid action in response. Although he must depart from "neutrality" (Hoffer, 1985) and the patient if that becomes necessary, in general, he should stay motionless and attentive, almost to the point of appearing unaffected by the storm. This is silently reassuring to the patient; a parent's non-anxious, non-retaliatory resolve in face of a child's temper tantrum is a developmental counterpart to such "containment." Another intervention useful in such circumstances is simply to name the overwhelming emotion. Katan (1961) made this point when she said that "verbalization leads to an increase of the controlling function of the ego over affects and drives" (p. 185). At times, addressing the patient by his first name during the emotional outburst gives him a cognitive handle for restabilization. Thus, calmly absorbing the affective spill, naming the emotion, and gently providing small cognitive anchors are the methods by which the therapist can bring the emotional flooding under control.

CONCLUDING REMARKS

In this contribution, we have elucidated the forms, antecedents, and consequences of violence in four settings: (i) domestic, (ii) criminal, (iii) political, and (iv) clinical. We have also addressed the societal and psychotherapeutic strategies aimed at reducing rage, hate, and violence. While we have cast our net wide, certain areas still remain unaddressed. These include the incidence, frequency, nature, and intensity of violence across the variables of (i) gender, (ii) life span, and (iii) culture. These are vast topics themselves and all we can do here is to briefly touch upon them in the hope that our comments will whet the readers' appetite for further study.

As far as gender is concerned, it is widely accepted that males are more violent than females (Caesar, 1988; Talman and Bennett, 1990; Hamberger and Hastings, 1991; Sugarman and Frankel, 1996). They commit more brutal crimes and more murders. The same applies to self-directed aggression. Women attempt suicide more often but men, prone to greater violence and having more access to firearms, end up killing themselves more often than women. The reasons for such gender-biased difference in the frequency and degree of violence are biopsychosocial in nature. Higher levels of testosterone in males contribute to their greater muscular strength and agility. Therefore, males, from childhood onward, are more prone to be motorically active and to discharge emotions via action. Greater amounts of aggression are needed for the "boy's dis-identification with the mother" (Greenson, 1968), and for a male child to avoid merger anxiety, sustain separateness, and form an authentic identity. Aggressiveness in men, whether in the form of ruthless competitiveness or in physical activity leading to intimidation of peers, is often upheld by the culture-at-large. Most, if not all, of the "superheroes" are males. And, then there is the greater availability of socially approved channels (e.g., the rough and tough of certain sports, military, war) which allow male aggression to flourish while subtly and not-so-subtly discouraging similar traits in women. Given all this, it is hardly surprising that men are more violent than women.

As far as the life span variable is concerned, violence can be seen at all ages though less so toward infancy and old age. At the beginning stage of life, neither motor coordination nor psychic agency are well established; this precludes outward displacement of aggression on the part of the infant. Moreover, the baby's existence is almost totally dependent upon caretakers and thus rage, even if it accrues, is mostly discharged upon itself. Later in childhood, violence, if it does erupt, takes the primitive forms of scratching and biting since access to more "sophisticated" tools of destructiveness (e.g., knives, guns) is limited. At the other end of life, too, one notices a certain diminution of violence. This is attributed to the overall decrease in the intensity of instinctual life, diminishing levels of hormones that contribute to aggressiveness, experience-caused "burn-out," and actual infirmity and growing weakness of the body. A paranoid worldview and cantankerous behavior might still prevail but physical discharge of aggression becomes less apparent.

Finally, there is the issue of cross-cultural variation in the prevalence of violence. While the tendency to be violent is hard-wired and ubiquitous, there does seem to be a difference in the degree and frequency of violent acts across cultures. Finer debates notwithstanding, a most convincing evidence for this assertion comes from the variability of murder rates across nations. With shame as patriotic American citizens, we acknowledge that ours is the worst nation in this regard. In 2016, the estimated murder rate in the United States was 5.3 murders per 100,000 people (Friedman, Grawert, and Cullen, 2017); this translates into approximately 17,000 individuals being killed in the span of those twelve months. Comparing this to the annual murder rates across the globe, reported in the 2015 statistics of the United Nations Office on Drugs and Crime, reveals considerable regional variations. The rate of murder is 1.58 per 100,000 in France (1017 murders per year), 1.36 per 100,000 in Israel (110 murders per year), 0.85 per 100,000 (682 murders per year) in Germany, 0.56 per 100,000 in the United Kingdom (594 murders per year), and 0.31 per 100,000 in Japan (395 murders per year), testifying to the implicit sociocultural foundations of overt aggression, destructiveness, fire-arm availability, and lethal violence. Hanging our head low, we admit that there is something quite "uncivilized" about our nation.

This brings us back full circle to where we started, namely at Freud's quoting an anonymous English author that the person who used a curse word instead of casting a spear was the founder of civilization. We find ourselves suddenly shame-faced, embarrassed, and timid. How can we report that our nation, the United States of America, has the highest murder rate in the world and the most firearm-related violence and yet declare itself to be a civilized—if not the most civilized—country? But bowing our heads in shame is hardly productive. Thinking, conceptualizing, conducting scientific research, and social activism that lead to curtailment of the mayhem all around us are better strategies. In order to improve the reality, we first have to acknowledge it and have to anchor our socio-clinical praxis in it. In other words, the ending of our discourse is actually a beginning of further, deeper, and more productive work vis-à-vis violence and its eradication.

Chapter 2

Learning the Difference between Hate and Violence

Kerry Kelly Novick

Babies *do* things that have a real impact on the environment—they smile, and, all being well, someone smiles back; they cry and someone offers milk; they reach and grab and throw. These actions build a store of real experience of effectance.[1] From the very beginning, babies in such good-enough circumstances learn to depend on an internal sequence of feelings that lead to actions that lead to gratifying results. That pleasure motivates babies to do more and try more. Jack Novick and I would describe those babies as using an "open-system" response (Novick and Novick, 2016) to the challenges of infancy.

Consider, however, babies whose actions do not evoke a relevant response, who do not feel effective in having an impact on the real world and the real people around them, who don't have opportunities for safe exploration and expansion. How are they to deal with frustration and helplessness? What avenues are open to them? If they can't exert any dependable realistic control over the people and things around them, if the people in their world are unavailable or inimical for some reason, they have to resort to magical means, to actions driven by beliefs that are not necessarily realistic. These are the babies we describe as finding a "closed-system" solution (Novick and Novick, 2016) to their predicament, striving to meet their basic, legitimate emotional needs as best they can.

In both these circumstances, the babies do not act alone. They are part of a complex network of relationships that either contribute to the smooth evolution of a sense of agency that starts in the body ego and is subsumed in the ego or thwart or distort that process, making realistic efforts feel increasingly futile. This way of thinking about earliest experience has always been part of a robust minority psychoanalytic tradition of a dual track model of development. But most psychoanalysts have been trained and work with a single-track model, further reinforced by political and intellectual pressure to focus only on intrapsychic unfolding and psychic reality, at the expense of knowledge, now firmly established across all scientific domains, that nature and nurture never operate in isolation, but always interact and affect each other. What happens psychically happens within a real body and a real brain; both influence and are influenced by the action of the environment, directly or through relationships. "Chicken and egg" is an inaccurate image, as the interdigitation of gene expression and the impact of experience happen simultaneously at the microscopic cellular and neuronal level, and in the micromoments of registration in the mind through links, networks, and memory traces.

So, we've established that babies use the environment's responses to them to construct internal models or schemata that link feelings or impulses with actions and effects. What about the next step? How do we learn the *difference* between feelings and actions? What can contribute to or interfere with the achievement of that crucial distinction that forms part of the core of the sense of self and separateness? In the context of our discussions in this volume, how can children learn to know their feelings of anger, resentment, rage, rivalry, suspicion, and hate, know what to do with them, and learn how to decide when to act on their feelings or not? What transforms an encompassing state of anger into an internal signal? What modulates the line from helplessness to anger to rage to hate?

> Two teenaged boys videotaped themselves.
>
> One said, "If you could see all the anger I've stored over the past four years."
>
> The other: "More rage. More rage. Keep building it on."
>
> The first: "Except for [my] parents, [my] extended family treated [me] like the runt of the litter. You made me what I am. You added to the rage. As far back as the Foothill Day Care Center, [I] hated the stuck-up kids who hated [me]. Being shy didn't help. I'm going to kill you all. You've been giving us shit for years." (*Time* magazine, 1999)

These are the words of Eric Harris and Dylan Klebold, the boys who killed their classmates and themselves at Columbine High School, now almost 20 years ago. We all feel an intense need to understand how these and the many similar terrible events since happened. We all have the sense that there is a virulent increase in violence in our society and we share a conviction that it is harming our children, just as powerfully as any terrible epidemic might. Both the disease and the cure, however, can seem as if they come from *outside* the child. And there are many determinants from the outside world that can indeed be reliably identified as risk factors. Poverty and deprivation, isolation, abuse, violence in the home, on the streets, in the media—these all play a role and all need to be addressed.

But we are psychoanalysts. What we do is think and look and listen to the *inner* worlds of children, adolescents, and adults and the *interaction* of these with outside experiences. In this way, we gain knowledge of the developmental challenges facing children as they grapple with both impulses from within and influences from without.

I would like to describe a little boy whom I will call "Eddie." He and his teenaged mother, "Sandra," lived in a residential center for two years, where complete care was provided, so they give us an approximation of a controlled experiment. Various of the known contributing factors to violence were eliminated by the setting; socioeconomic issues of poverty and class, deprivation, ongoing trauma, family pressures, ignorance, isolation, and acute medical or psychiatric problems played little direct role as Eddie's development progressed.

We first met Eddie and Sandra when Eddie was only four weeks old. They had come to live in a long-term residential program for teenage mothers and their babies, which was designed by psychoanalysts to help young mothers with no other resources to keep their babies and bond with them. Sandra had had a very difficult life. She and her sister had been abused physically and sexually in childhood. When she was eight, Sandra had witnessed a murder. She became pregnant at 16 with Eddie just after her beloved older brother was sent to prison for murdering a neighbor girl who was Sandra's age. Sandra was tough and smart, and determined to make a better life for herself and her son. Her childhood experiences gave her clear ideas of what she wanted to avoid. They also left her with many worries about what to do with her own angry impulses and sexual wishes. On the one hand, Sandra longed for a strong man to take care of her and protect her from harm; on the other hand, she saw men as uncontrollable killers, whose sexuality was dangerous and unpredictable.

One solution Sandra found was to try to be self-sufficient, so she wouldn't need a man, and then wouldn't be exposed to the dangers they represented. But this didn't help her much with her own angry feelings. Another solution was to put the feelings outside herself, that is, to externalize them. Then she could see others as the angry ones and feel entitled to attack them. In the neighborhood where she grew up, the angriest ones were the men, who got everything they wanted by force. When she had a boy child, he became the repository of Sandra's bad feelings. In a film of a feeding when Eddie was a month old, he and Sandra gazed at each other, and she smiled at him. She also called him names that attributed her own wishes to him, like "greedy pig." In the next few months, she slapped his hands when he reached for things, and always told him, "You're bad."

Sitting on the floor with lots of toys when Eddie was eight months old, Sandra could not seem to let him explore and enjoy—she interrupted every play sequence as soon as Eddie showed signs of excitement and involvement. Sandra seemed afraid that things would get out of control. Many people would dismiss Sandra's behavior with Eddie as "just ordinary teasing," and she certainly did not blatantly mistreat him. But the child psychoanalysts involved in the residential program were concerned about Sandra's disregard of Eddie's individuality, and the hostility implied in her calling him names, interrupting him at every turn, and attributing her bad qualities to him (Campbell et al., 1995).

It was actually Sandra who had trouble staying in control of her own impulses. Playing catch with a beach ball when Eddie was a year old, they were both having fun, and Eddie crowed with delight each time he caught the ball and returned it to his mother. Then she accidentally hit Eddie's head with the ball. Sandra went on to bounce it off Eddie's head repeatedly, calling him "Old man, fat belly." At first he looked bewildered. But then Eddie began to hit himself in the head with both hands.

This was a crucial transition for Eddie. He moved from being the helpless victim of Sandra's attack on him and her disruption of his pleasure in competent mastery to actively taking in the aggression, accepting her attribution of the angry parts of herself. The more Sandra assigned her own anger, excitement, and neediness to Eddie, the more aggressive he began to look. In addition, Sandra's frustration of his normal exploration and assertion increasingly evoked an angry response. Eddie had more and more anger to deal with as his mother thwarted, rather than facilitated, his attempts to master his world. As he grew into toddlerhood and there was still no help available to learn what to do with his angry feelings, Eddie in turn began to dump them outside. He became the aggressor, biting other children in the nursery and provoking his mother by refusing to make eye contact with her when they sat down for a snack together.

Although Eddie spent his first years in a benign and sheltered environment, Sandra's lifelong experiences had a powerful impact on the early formation of his personality. We might understand this as an example of a parent's personality, shaped as it is by forces from inside and outside, being the most important component of a child's environment in the early years. Sandra and Eddie were living in a carefully planned residential setting, with many different educational and support services. But Sandra needed more than education and nice people around her to change. She needed therapy as well, which takes time. During that time, Eddie absorbed the world through the filter of his mother's difficulties and reacted by developing his own troubles with aggression. Thus, the early foundation of his personality was patterned by Sandra's troubles.

Life offers many challenges from the very beginning, with opportunities for mastery or failure. If a child is born with disabilities or deficiencies, or if the important people in his life are inadequate in some way, that child will be vulnerable to being overwhelmed from within or without. When babies' feelings are not modulated through assistance from parents, they feel helpless. If the outside world is overstimulating or terrifying, neglectful or assaultive, babies feel helpless. With good-enough equipment and good-enough parenting, babies can master their experience. Without that support, they find unhealthy ways to survive and to attempt to feel good about themselves. They try to master overwhelming experience by getting rid of the bad feelings as soon as possible. In clinical work, Jack Novick and I have come to describe this process of attempted mastery as involving two possible systems of self-regulation.

Over the past fifty years, as we have studied destructive and self-destructive behavior in children, adolescents and adults, we have found it useful to describe these outcomes in terms of two possible systems of self-regulation and conflict resolution, available throughout the life cycle. One we have described as the "open system." In open-system functioning, the challenges of life are met in a reality-attuned way, which leads to feelings of competence, effectance, and joy. The essence of this system is captured in Eddie's loving gaze and his effective sucking, in his crow of delight as he catches and throws the ball. We all took pleasure in watching his play. In the open system, good feelings come from adaptive interactions with others. The little child can be sensitive to the feelings of others, can accept reality constraints, and his good feelings of competence and self-worth give him confidence to explore the world of people and things.

Open-system functioning in the elementary school years is marked by a capacity to accept rules and enjoy learning from adults and peers. Pleasure comes from mastery and growth of bodily, cognitive, and emotional skills. At adolescence, open-system functioning allows the teenager to meet the many challenges of new demands with confidence and an increased capacity to become a good, validating parent to himself.

Under stress from internal or external sources, anyone at any time can resort to a different way of functioning, that is, according to a "closed system." Then self-esteem is maintained by a magical belief in omnipotent power to control others. A feature of closed-system functioning is the use of externalization, followed by attack. Original victimization is turned into active provocation of attack or habitual experience of being mistreated. As a victim, the person feels entitled to break societal rules and attack others. Again, Eddie gives us a vivid portrayal of the shift from open-system loving to closed-system externalization, provocation, and attack. He has made his mother helpless and angry and he feels justified in cutting her dead. The movement is from assertion, that is frustrated, to anger and aggression, which, if not transformed into signal affect, but left as an intense and overwhelming state of helplessness, easily slides into sadism and hate. As we learned from Sandra's therapy and could see in Eddie's escalating aggression, they were both establishing a vicious cycle, in which the destruction of their love for each other played a crucial role. Once love is swept away, the other person can be objectified and dehumanized, and then the violence of externalizing parts of oneself on to another person becomes possible.

Externalization is a way to avoid the feeling of helplessness that comes with being overwhelmed by impulses or emotions. Sandra needed to externalize greedy, messy, incompetent, and aggressive aspects of her personality on to Eddie. He maintained his attachment to her by taking these in and identifying with the aggressor, turning the violence on himself and others. When the outside world, in its reaction, confirms the belief that feelings really are destructively powerful and can overwhelm, damage, or kill, the child gets the message that his anger is a fast and powerful solution to his helplessness. The stage is then set for the development of a full-blown power relationship. His self-regulation and his self-esteem already depend on proving his power to control the other person.

We can see this happening in the course of the films that were taken as part of a developmental record for each mother and child in the program: there is a sharp contrast between Eddie's attentive gaze as his mother enjoyed feeding him at one month of age and their aversion and inability to look at each other during a snack when he was fifteen months. They had become blind to each other as beloved individuals. Jack Novick and I have described this "soul blindness" as a condition for externalization and other assaults, ranging from bullying in school to ethnic cleansing and suicidal terrorist murders of civilians (Novick and Novick, 2005). During the next stage of the cycle, love itself becomes the danger, leaving one prey to being a helpless victim or the sufferer of overwhelming shame and guilt, and so it is warded off and rage and hate become the predominant motivators and protections of the personality.

The factors leading to violent actions are manifold and spring from all levels of development. What our experience with Sandra and Eddie and other young children shows us, however, is the centrality of the experience of helplessness and rage. Helplessness is an intolerable condition, from which people seek immediate escape. Without internal or external supports, a readily available option is a closed-system, omnipotent response, leading to the sequence we saw in Sandra and Eddie's interaction—helplessness, externalization, internalization, and attack.

If an open-system, alternative, path is not found by the time a child goes to school, the sequence will repeat itself in all the child's interactions—in provocative confrontations with teachers and bullying or being bullied on the playground. This is the pattern that gets reinforced by videogames and movies that derive from schoolchild fantasies of easy, violent, and quick solutions to problems. In a shooting tragedy in Flint, Michigan, in 2000, two six-year-olds had an argument in the schoolyard. The little boy's father was in jail, the boy's mother had abandoned him, his caretakers were unreliable and unavailable, and he had never had good examples of mastering feelings and impulses or resolving conflicts. He was helpless to get his needs met, and the grown-ups around him had no resources. He was alone with his hurt and anger and helplessness, both at home and in relation to his classmate. It may be that he externalized all these feelings on to the available little girl. Blaming her for his helplessness and pain, wanting to get rid of those unbearable feelings, he took his uncle's gun, and, at school the next day, enacted a scene he had seen repeatedly at home and on TV. He shot six-year-old Kayla through the heart and killed her. Violence had become his way of feeling strong and good about himself.

By the age of six, most children know the difference between right and wrong. But this cognitive understanding is easily swept away by helplessness and rage. As children reach school age, they enter the wider world of friends, school, and new adults. There is now a possibility to offer a child support for consolidation of open-system, competent functioning or supply new alternatives to those children who have so far known only the closed cycle of helplessness and violence.

By the teenage years violent death reaches crisis proportions. Murder and suicide are the second and third leading causes of death for those between the ages of twelve and twenty-one, with car accidents the first. Murder and suicide, however, belong together, in that the rates of each rise and fall with each other, and because they share the same underlying dynamic. Similarly, many fatal adolescent car crashes are actually murder/suicides.

Jack Novick and I have studied medically serious adolescent suicide attempts for many years. We have invariably found that the precipitant was a feeling of desperate helplessness, which was then pushed away by rageful, vindictive, destructive behavior that makes others the helpless ones. Suicidal teenagers follow a sequence of escalating helplessness, blaming, and attack on others via self-destruction. For instance, with a young woman, whom we'll call "Mary," her older brother repeatedly raped her in the upstairs bedroom. Her mother, obsessively cleaning house downstairs, remained oblivious. Mary felt she had no recourse, drove her mother's new car off a cliff and nearly died. Her suicide attempt left her parents bewildered and helpless.

Research on accelerating recruitment of American youngsters to violent neo-Nazi white supremacist groups stresses the causative role of economic helplessness. Areas of economic depression, where plants have closed and unemployment has risen, have become prime sources of fresh recruits. Extremist groups and gangs offer the helpless teenager an easy solution, an externalization of blame on the usual scapegoats. All terrorist groups seem to follow a similar pattern of constructing an omnipotent belief system that compensates for feelings of helplessness. The Columbine boys referred repeatedly in their videotapes to their hatred and fear of blacks, Jews, and other minorities. We don't know the specific sources of Dylan Klebold's and Eric Harris' helplessness, but the longstanding nature of their troubles, their externalized blaming, and their sense of license for violence against others and themselves are evident. They rendered a whole community helpless and the ripples continue.

What can counter this escalating spiral of hate? Remember Eddie's loving gaze as a newborn, his curiosity in play, his joyful exuberance playing ball—love, joy, competence, creativity, and pleasure in the parent-child relationship are interacting and mutually reinforcing factors to absorb and transform rage. It is an ongoing task to consolidate these factors in the developing personality, but this is the best protection against the possibility of later violence. Social supports through schools and community institutions for both parents and children consolidate the capacity for empathy, the sense of self-worth, and the respect for other individuals that are crucial inoculations against the spread of unchecked violence.

When I describe two systems of conflict resolution, one open to feelings of effectance, competence, love and joy, the other, closed system, characterized by helplessness and rage, I do not mean to imply that it is an easy matter to choose between the two. No amount of education or behavior modification alone will convince a traumatized child that there is safety in other pathways than violence. Violence does provide an illusion of safety, a quick and easy apparent solution to very complex problems. In our work we have emphasized that violence is not pathology, but a *solution* that stems from a closed, omnipotent belief system.

We should recognize that we, as parents, teachers, citizens, and mental health professionals, can also feel helpless and so need to counter our own wishes for a simple solution. Some elements of a multifaceted solution are straightforward, such as gun control. Great Britain, with large ethnic minorities, overcrowding, extreme income disparities, and social unrest among unemployed youths, has no handguns and has an annual murder rate equal to one day in Detroit. We have to recognize that those who oppose gun controls may be living according to a closed, omnipotent belief in the efficacy of violence as the only protection against their helplessness in the face of unfamiliar or unknown dangers.

Other elements are more complex. The road is long and demands goodwill, intelligence, persistence and hard work from all. In her psychoanalytic psychotherapy, Sandra gained understanding of her own struggles with anger, and only then was she better able to see Eddie as a person in his own right and regain her love for him. With the efforts of a supportive community of peers, older adults, teachers, and therapists, she learned to help him own his feelings, put them into words, and communicate his needs. Eddie's biting and angry withdrawal diminished. Eddie's mother came to her task handicapped by her own past. Its effects were visible in Eddie's development. With support and therapeutic help, Sandra was able to vanquish the worst of her demons, go on to college, and support Eddie's growth emotionally and practically. The intergenerational cycle of violence was broken.

There is another important element to address if we are to approach these complex problems realistically. At some point in each of the developmental film clips, either Sandra or Eddie or both looked at the filmmaker. Initially, those of us working on the project were inclined to attribute this to embarrassment or curiosity, and there may have been some of each. But both Sandra and Eddie were used to this familiar person filming them and other pairs around the cottage and rarely paid him much attention. What *was* unusual about the filming situation was that it was the only time in which interactions were allowed to continue without interruption, no matter what their nature. In other words, unlike all other staff, the cameraman in this context played the role of a passive bystander.

The role of the bystander is very important in understanding hostile actions and power relationships (Twemlow, 2000). The perpetrator of violence demands that the bystander actively condone or at least passively allow abuse. This collusion on the part of the bystander makes the victim feel even more helpless and ready to resort to equally destructive or self-attacking behavior to save himself. The staff of the residential center realized retrospectively that the filming was the only situation of collusive bystanding in the program, since everyone usually responded quickly to avert roughness or abusive interactions, both to stop the particular event and to forestall the escalation that comes from the collusion of the passive bystander.

In discussions of early child development, and in applications of the two systems ideas to political functioning, we have pointed out that the hostile, omnipotent belief that one can actually do whatever one wishes can only develop and be maintained if the environment colludes in some way. This may start in infancy when a parent tries to control a baby unduly and is in turn tyrannized by the child. Often one parent is the sadistic perpetrator in the power struggle and the child is the victim, while the other parent is either psychologically or physically absent, as was the case with Eddie. The absence of an alternative in the person of another parent functions as the collusion of the bystander. There may be a similar pattern when a patient has drawn a therapist into a sadomasochistic interaction, and a supervisor fails to intervene actively, but remains a neutral or helpless bystander, thus becoming dynamically involved in the perverse relationship at a distance.

This pattern of enmeshment in sadomasochistic functioning gets repeated in social relationships in the preschool and school years. The child who has been trapped without recourse in a hostile power struggle in a family relationship can become a bully who victimizes others and demands the active or passive collusion of others including adults. Children who have not been helped to develop mastery of their feelings, who don't have strong "waiting muscles, who don't have models for good feelings from competent functioning, will seek high status through the debasement of others" (Novick and Novick, 2010). Excitement is achieved from the helplessness of others and maintained by demanding the admiration of bystanders too frightened to challenge the bully. The "good" children feel unprotected and withdraw into isolation or the protection of groups that can easily become exclusive cliques.

All of this can make adults feel helpless for a number of reasons. It is hard to empathize with the cruelty and brutality of a bully—it makes us want to withdraw too. Bullies are excited by their victims' pain and humiliation. It is not enough for them to establish dominance; they are driven to repeat the attacks. To people with a functioning conscience, this behavior makes no sense. It also evokes rage in us, with the consequent impulse to retaliate in kind, to show the bully what it feels like. Most of us are shocked by such reactions in ourselves, especially when they are directed against children or the patients we are trying to help. One response can be to shut ourselves down, which results in withdrawal and passivity.

Reactive rage is sometimes channeled into escalating institutional punitiveness, with proliferating rules and rigidity, harsh automatic sentences or building more prisons. "Zero tolerance" is a crucial first step, but if this is all that is done, the punishments and sanctions can escalate, rather than reduce, the violence. The bully comes from and lives in a mental world of violence and power struggles. He expects and seeks a violent reaction, whether in life or in treatment. Being the victim of retaliation confirms his power and justifies to him his own escalating and persistent violence. This creates a terrible difficulty for the therapists, teachers, parents, and legislators trying to craft a constructive remedy. What are we to do?

First we have to accept responsibility. We must recognize that violence is part of a psychological and social system of externalization, blame, and attack. In such a closed system of functioning, solutions are magically quick and easy—hence the appeal of violence. In an open system, we acknowledge complexity. Most human behavior is complex and multi-determined. Therefore, it demands multimodal intervention for effective change. When a child is violent or is the victim of violence, no one person or institution is to blame. We are all responsible. Lasting change will require input from everyone—from the child, the family, the community, teachers, schools, police, courts, the medical and psychological professionals, academic and clinical research, the legal system, and legislators at all levels. Tupac Shakur, a rap artist and composer murdered at 25, said "I am society's child. This is how they made me and now I'm sayin' what's on my mind and they don't want that. This is what you made me, America."

Second, we must each act despite the complexity. Anything you do will have some effect. Whenever you refuse to go along with teasing or discrimination; whenever a teacher insists that two children find a way to resolve differences; whenever we demand that principals or administrators use their authority to back up teachers or agency workers; whenever you give and expect respectful interchange with peers and colleagues, parents and children; whenever you make the effort to help someone else; whenever you try to understand someone very different from yourself; whenever we stay with our conviction that inner roots of violence are discoverable—the list goes on. All of these actions in fact have a double effect. They affect each person involved and they also encourage similar actions in others. Social inspiration opposes social intimidation. Each individual can be a leader, in all the places we work and live, including the consulting room, where our collaborative and respectful alliances with patients and families carry a powerful message.

Third, we must intervene early and keep at it. The sooner we get involved, the more effective we can be. Parents who have learned not to shake their baby will teach him to take good care of himself, which will equip him to stand up to bullies. Parents who have learned to listen to and talk to their toddler are modeling essential respect, sowing the seeds of the capacity to negotiate and compromise. Early intervention, the very idea of which stems from psychoanalytic understanding of personality development, is humanly, socially, and financially economical. The sooner we all work to create a culture in which no one feels it is more comfortable and acceptable to stand by and do nothing, the sooner we will never have to feel that what we provide is too little, too late. These are the ideas that inspired a group of us to start the nonprofit Allen Creek Preschool in Ann Arbor, Michigan, where we can begin work with pregnant parents, then parents and infants, and follow through the stages of development up to elementary school. We support young children and their families from all backgrounds by reinforcing the positive, protective factors in their lives and helping them find competent and loving open-system ways to overcome the inevitable risk factors and difficulties of each phase of development.

Fourth, we can work to make our professional training and practice function in an open system of self-regulation and conflict resolution. When patients seek our help, they are struggling to feel better. A major way patients have found to restore self-esteem and balance is to externalize helplessness, as we saw with Sandra and then with Eddie. This also applies in treatment, where the patient seeks to render the therapist helpless.

The same dynamic can then arise in the supervisee/supervisor relationship, where the supervisee gets rid of the unbearable feeling of futility by either making the supervisor helpless or submitting in enthralled compliance to an omniscient supervisor. The supervisor too is in a risky predicament. There is great potential for amplified helplessness—the supervisor is hearing material at a remove, shaped by the patient's resistances and externalizations, compounded perhaps by the therapist's inexperience or limitations or conflicts. The overarching context for these dynamics is a power relationship, with all that entails in terms of potential for abuse.

A two-systems understanding of the supervisory relationship leads to an effort to maintain open-system interaction, with effective collaboration and realistic use of the strengths and limitations of each party. The effort is to reverse the chain reaction that can be initiated when a patient draws the therapist into a sadomasochistic externalizing relationship. The supervisor starts by checking his or her own affective reaction to the presentation of the treatment material—is it overwhelming? Does it engender over-certainty? Because open-system understanding is complex and takes time, these feelings alert the supervisor to the need to share responsibility with the therapist for working gradually through a sequence that addresses the patient's needs on many levels.

Violent and/or abused patients are not going to give up violence, either as perpetrators or victims, without a viable alternative. Just as supervisor and supervisee must achieve an alternative to an authoritarian relationship in collaboration and mutual support for tolerance of frustration and ambiguity, so it is helpful for the therapist to have a mental model of a sequence of interventions that will eventually offer the patient a choice of responses to conflict or overwhelming trauma. With violent and/or abused patients, it is important first to *identify the legitimate needs being served* by their sadomasochistic functioning. Only then can the therapist begin with the patient to *measure the cost* of meeting those needs in that way. Over time, *alternatives can be generated* that can meet essential needs, resolve conflicts, and promote self-regulation, with consequent improvement in self-esteem.

The last sequence in the films of Eddie and Sandra was taken when Eddie was nineteen months old, four months after the snack time when he had hatefully blotted her out, turning stonily away from eye contact and any conversational overtures she made. In the final film, as he plays with his mom, sharing a toy that makes animal noises, we see them beginning to rebuild attunement and mutual enjoyment, working toward an alternative loving relationship with each other that will strengthen them both and influence others in the same direction.

NOTE

1. While I take responsibility for this articulation, the ideas in this chapter spring from thinking and writing over the past 50 years with Jack Novick. The reference list details resources for learning more about the evolution of our ideas.

Chapter 3

Rage, Violence, and Terrorism

Ann G. Smolen

Kerry Novick begins her presentation by explaining when life is "good-enough," babies are able to make use of what the Kerry and her husband, Jack Novick call an "open-system" response to the normal disruptions and frustrations of parent-child interactions. Kerry then turns her attention to the many parents, infants, and children who unfortunately, face more difficult circumstances. These infants learn very early and very quickly that their world is not a safe place. Kerry states: "These babies we describe as finding a 'closed-system' solution to their predicament." Kerry goes on to say that of course the baby is not acting in isolation, but rather all interactions are co-created. In her newest book, *Freedom To Choose: Two Systems of Self-Regulation* (2016), co-authored with Jack Novick, Kerry explains: "when faced with overwhelming experiences, whether they originate from internal or external events, all people throughout life must find some way to feel good" (p. 3). Kerry asks several valuable questions: "What is the difference between feelings and actions?" And: "What modulates the line from helplessness to anger and rage?" I would add a further question: "What causes rage to turn into violent acts of terrorism?" Most importantly, Kerry asks: "How can children learn to know their feelings of anger, resentment, rage, rivalry, suspicion, and hate, know what to do with them, and learn how to decide when to act on their feelings or not?"

Kerry brilliantly demonstrates, answering her own questions for us, showing us what helps mothers and children move from a pathological "closed-system" of interacting, to a healthier, more adaptive "open-system." She tells us "Sandra's" story of horrendous abuse and neglect and how both Sandra and Eddie found themselves in hopeless situations, which then led to anger and rage and maladaptive behaviors. The Novicks explain their "open-and-closed system" response as two ways to resolve conflict and attend to self-regulation. The "open-system" response is "attuned to reality and characterized by joy, competence, and creativity," while the "closed-system" response "avoids reality and is characterized by sadomasochism, omnipotence, and stasis" (p. 5). Eddie was lucky because he and his mother benefited from an analytic intervention when he was an infant. Kerry, without a doubt, demonstrates that early intervention with both the mother and child can make all the difference. I have seen this in my own work with homeless mothers and their children.

Kerry reminds us about Eric Harris and Dylan Klebold, the two adolescent boys who went on a killing rampage at Columbine High School almost 20 years ago. What brought these children to that terrible place where their murderous thoughts and feelings were acted out? Why were they stuck in what the Novicks call a "closed-system" of being in the world? These boys became child terrorists. Kerry noted that we would never know why these boys did what they did. If either of these boys had entered into treatment as younger children, what would that have looked like? Do we see children such as these in our offices? I am going to share with you my work with two boys. The first was what I would call a failed treatment, the second treatment successful.

CASE # 1: BARNARD

Fourteen-year-old Bernard, is the highly revered son in a family of many sisters. On the surface, Bernard's history seems surprisingly uneventful. His parent's professional and financial successes have allowed Barnard every opportunity: the best schools, musical instrument lessons, sports, and a home with every amenity imaginable. Bernard's father is often absent, away on business trips for weeks at a time. His mother, while the emotional core of the family, is intrusive and controlling in her interactions with her only son. His mother described an angelic little boy who had suddenly gone rotten.

So what went wrong? Why was Bernard sullen, belligerent, rude, and most of all arrogant? At age 12, Bernard began spending most of his time alone in his room. Over the next two years, his behavior worsened. He was disrespectful toward his parents, pouring the majority of his rage onto his mother, spitting out venomous verbiage. His mother described his behavior toward herself and Bernard's sisters as "deplorable and torturous."

Bernard slunk into my office, his eyes darting around anxiously, taking in his surroundings. I found myself working very hard to connect with him to no avail. In the early weeks, Bernard saw me as an advocate as I was able to help his mother understand that an adolescent boy needs privacy (she now allowed him to close his bedroom door) and gain some autonomy (she began to let him venture out on his skateboard and bike). In retrospect, perhaps, this parental intervention was a mistake because Bernard began to hate me as his rage overwhelmed both of us. He could not tolerate receiving anything nice or good from me, just as he could not accept anything good from his mother. I immediately became the over-bearing intrusive mother in the transference to be hated and despised. I was hoping to develop a positive transference with Bernard knowing all too well what was to come, however only negative feelings persisted.

Each session was worse than the preceding one. Now that he had what he wanted from me—to get his way with his mother—he no longer had any use for me. He communicated his rage through physical acting-out behaviors. In every session, he would do one or several of the following: (1) break all of the light bulbs in my lamps by shaking the lamps; (2) cut up psychoanalytic brochures in my waiting room; (3) toss my newly upholstered chair across my office; (4) put his dirty shoes all over my newly upholstered furniture; (5) try to start a fire by playing with the lamp cord in the electrical outlet, making sparks; (6) in my playroom, throw glass marbles so hard against the wall that many shattered; (7) bring in my office food and eat it, dropping crumbs and wiping his sticky fingers on the furniture. It goes without saying that I stopped all of these disruptive behaviors and attempted to translate his behaviors into words and attempted to understand the meaning behind the behaviors. I also sought consultation in order to continue to try to reach this boy, but also to sort out my countertransference. I was beginning to hate him as he hated me.

The day after televised horrific terrorist attacks in Paris, Bernard began his session animated and uncharacteristically talkative. Earlier in the day, his mother had left me a voice message despairingly describing how Bernard's treatment of his sisters had worsened and he was "terrorizing" the family. In his session, Bernard gave an oration emphatically declaring that the terrorists were not to be blamed for their murderous behaviors because they were indoctrinated, "that is how they were brought up to think, it isn't personal, it's their political beliefs." I wondered aloud about the innocent people who were murdered and their families who were left behind to suffer in grief, and the senselessness of the terrorist acts. He again stated that none of that mattered because the terrorists were groomed to not care about individuals. They did what they did for the greater good. At that point, I remembered his mother's earlier message to me and I shared with Bernard that his mother felt he was terrorizing his family and she was extremely concerned about him. I asked him why he was acting like a terrorist, because surely that was not how he was being brought up. He got up and stormed out of my office.

This vignette is embarrassing to confess as I certainly was not at my analytic best, to say the least. Bernard was trying to tell me about himself in displacement and I was so overcome by my countertransference and by my own dismay over what had transpired in Paris that I was not able to meet him in his displacement. I could not stay in the "play," and Bernard could not tolerate the reality. Bernard's behaviors worsened. I spent most of our sessions stopping him from destroying my property. Once he stopped acting out physically, he lashed out verbally degrading me, stating how stupid I am and how I could never be a help to him because of my low intelligence. I was now the cause of all of his problems. He claimed that if he no longer had to come see me all would be well. He had no memory of what had brought him into therapy in the first place, and could not tolerate any attempt at exploring the multiple meanings that were motivating his hostile, arrogant behaviors. When summer came, Bernard left treatment to travel through Europe with a teen group. He did not return in the fall.

CASE 2: DAVID

I nicknamed five-year-old David "my angriest little boy." He was a force to be reckoned with. His divorced parents brought him to me because they could no longer tolerate his outlandish behaviors. He kicked, screamed, hit, stole, and hid his mother's belongings, broke household items, shouted obscenities at both of his parents, and punched his father in his penis. His mother was convinced he would become a drug addict and be in jail by the time he was an adolescent. In my meetings with David's parents, my office became a warzone. When both parents were present, the sessions quickly dissolved into contemptuous name calling by the father as David's mother dissolved into a sea of angry tears.

When I was in my office behind double doors and two sound machines, I heard him arriving. It sounded as if someone was throwing large heavy objects against the hallway walls and then against my waiting room walls. Within seconds, five-year-old, tiny for his age, David had turned off the sound machines, switched the channel on the radio, and changed the time on my clock. Children's books that I keep in a basket were strewn across the room and he was hiding under the couch. He easily separated from his mother who gave me an exasperated look as if to say "he is your problem now." David proceeded to continue his path of destruction in my office. I explained to David that I had few rules but there were two very important rules: (1) nobody is allowed to break my things on purpose, (2) nobody is allowed to hurt me. David continued to try to break my belongings and stated: "I don't care. I hate your things. I don't care about you or your things. I can do whatever I want to." Certainly, there was defiance in his actions, but he was telling me how out of control he felt. I decided at that moment, that even though it was exhausting for me, and seemed like I was not helping him to control his feelings, I allowed him to make gigantic, huge messes in my playroom.

Four sessions per week for over a year, David "stole" special objects that I keep in my adult office and hid them in my playroom. I would say: "Oh my, you have taken my very special shell, and have hidden it so well that it will take me days to find it. I will have to spend so much time looking for it and all that time I will be thinking of you and remembering our time together." David would turn away from me in an effort to hide his smile. At first, he smirked and laughed at me in a demeaning arrogant fashion as if to say, "You fool, I can make you do anything I want." Soon, it evolved into a smile of genuine pleasure that I would spend time thinking of and remembering him. In every session, he would run into my office and immediately look for the object he had hidden to make sure I had kept my word and kept him in mind.

His play was chaotic, dumping baskets of Legos, baskets of small cars, baskets of army figures, baskets of whatever I had. I would interpret his messes, showing him I would do my best to understand his inner feelings of chaos and help him put words to his actions. He refused to help me clean up his mess, arrogantly claiming that he sure didn't have to do that, because he didn't care how I felt ever!! I would reply: "Wow! This sure is a big mess. You really want me to spend so much time thinking about you because it will take me a long time to clean this up after you go home and all that time I will be thinking about you and thinking about all these messy difficult feelings you are having."

During this time, I was also meeting with David's parents separately on a regular basis. Over time, they began to feel heard and cared about by me; gradually they both began to listen to what I had to offer about David and their parenting began to change. Over the next two years, David's play became more contained and organized (of course I am greatly condensing his treatment here). He no longer needed to hide my belongings; stealing and hiding his mother's things also stopped. Instead of punishing David's unacceptable behaviors, his mother began to provide limits and boundaries and to validate the difficult feelings that were motivating the behaviors. In his sessions, when home life was challenging or he became anxious over schoolwork, he would once again regress to making huge messes with one difference: he could tell me what he was feeling after making the mess, and best of all, he offered to clean it up; we would do that together. I no longer thought of David as "my angriest little boy." After a two-week vacation, David's mother emailed me the following statement from David: "I don't know how Dr. Ann does it. I think she must have magic because all we do is play and I feel better."

THEORETICAL DISCUSSION

Over the last century, and especially since the Internet and social media explosion, parents were and are confused as to how and when to set limits. In the early 1900s:

> "Children were afraid to lose their parent's love; by the end of the century, at least in the United States, it was parents who seemed afraid they would lose their children's love. Parents not only feared the neurotic consequences of repressing their children; even more, they feared loss and any reproach from their children if they set standards, made demands, or invoked any consequences of behavior." (Novick and Novick, 2014, p. 443)

A majority of children no longer present for treatment with what analysts describe as classical neurotic symptoms. Instead, we are seeing children who experience difficulties in regulation and often exhibit defiant and oppositional behaviors at home and at school. Parents complain that they feel powerless and cannot help their children attend to homework, behave at mealtime, and settle into bed at night. "In the popular view, psychoanalysis did not seem to offer anything useful; indeed, it seemed to have created a monster" (Novick and Novick, 2014, p. 443). Psychoanalytic theory postulates that the infant is born omnipotent and slowly and unwillingly accepts reality. The Novicks argue that omnipotence is not normal, but rather "it is a defensive, compensatory belief, generated as a sometimes necessary response to the trauma of the failure of reality" (Novick and Novick, 2014, p. 444). The Novicks are convinced that omnipotence is not a part of normal development; in fact, they believe the complete opposite. In their view, the presence of omnipotence is a red flag and points to a pathological resolution to conflict. "Rather than the classical view that the failure of omnipotence forces the child to turn to reality, we suggest that it is the failure of reality that forces a child, at any point in development, to turn to closed-system omnipotent solutions, resulting in self-centered, entitled function" (Novick and Novick, 2014, p. 446).

More and more, child analysts are seeing children who are extremely anxious and out of control. Like Bernard, some of these children have been coddled and treated as "special." These children are entitled, grandiose, and arrogant. Like Bernard and David, these children have resorted to a "closed-system" of functioning. Their fragile "self-esteem is maintained by a magical belief in omnipotent power to control others."

DISCUSSION OF THE CASES

Both of the children that I described seemed to feel entitled "to be demanding and derogatory toward others" (Horney, 1945, p. 167). Unfortunately, Bernard's treatment ended prematurely and was not successful. The only way Bernard could figure out how to help himself feel better was to claim malicious victory over others by his demeaning and nasty thoughts and behaviors. He chose a "closed-system." It seemed to me that Bernard thought he was successful in fooling others into thinking he was superior to them, while in reality, Barnard was terrified that everyone would know the truth and see that he possessed faults, and had limitations. He had to guard against this sense of helplessness and humiliation at all costs as he believed that he could control others.

In the clinical vignette, where hate in the countertransference got the better of me, and I almost literally called Bernard a terrorist, his "protective layer of invulnerability" was pierced and he could not allow himself to tolerate the pain, so he fled. "Self-hate is always cruel and merciless" (Horney, 1955, p. 207). Bernard hated in others exactly what he despised in himself. Kerry aptly points out that "it is hard to empathize with cruelty and brutality of a bully–it makes us want to withdraw too" (Novick, 2017, p. 8). When Bernard defended the terrorists, I experienced strong negative feelings and retaliated. Kerry urges all of us to accept responsibility, acknowledge the complexity, and I would add, we need to find that place of empathy in order to help.

Both Bernard and David had seriously compromised abilities to develop healthy self-esteem. Both had developed rigid coping mechanisms resulting in an omnipotent sense of self. These children kept feelings of sadness at bay, making use of grandiosity to communicate to themselves and the world that they did not need anyone. Bernard and David both had serious difficulties in expressing love or gratitude, and displayed a disinterest in others. Both boys devalued others in an effort to maintain a stable sense of self. In the therapeutic relationship with me, both children played out their relentless attempts to remain disengaged, fearful that dependency and warm loving feelings might lead them to experience themselves as powerless and helpless. Over time, David was able to allow his rageful, narcissistic defenses to peel away, revealing new healthier coping mechanisms and defenses. As the Novicks emphasize: there are "two modes of conflict resolution and self-regulation, each of which is a possible response to conflict at any point in development" (Novick and Novick, 2016, p. 6). As David's treatment progressed, both he and his mother were better able to choose an "open-system" response.

PARTING THOUGHTS

The cases of Bernard and David demonstrate how pathological family configurations and dynamics can derail normal narcissistic development and result in children and adolescents who resort to omnipotence in order to cope with their world. These children are forced to choose a "closed-system" way of functioning. David, at the young age of five was already acting out his overwhelming rage as it turned into five-year-old violence. Bernard, an adolescent, was acting on his rage by becoming a bully as he terrorized his family and me. "Bullies are excited by their victims' pain and humiliation. It is not enough for them to establish dominance; they are driven to repeat attacks" (Novick, 2017, p. 8). These children are difficult to engage with and stimulate intense countertransference in the analyst, yet with patience and perseverance, and especially work with parents who engage in the treatment, these children can get back on the path to normal development. Kerry Novick has demonstrated strikingly and convincingly how analytic interventions with traumatized mothers and infants made a huge difference for her patients, Sandra and Eddie. Clearly, as Kerry has told us: "the sooner we get involved, the more effective we can be" (Novick, 2017, p. 9). I have seen that in my own work with children such as David, and in my work with homeless mothers and their babies.

Chapter 4

Gods Do Not Negotiate

A Psycho-Historical Look at Terrorism

Vamık D. Volkan

In today's world, almost daily, we are exposed to news of terrorism, mostly carried out by extreme fundamentalist Islamic terrorist groups or lone wolves linked to them. History informs us about many instances of killing in the name of religion. The Zealots, the Assassins and the Thuggees were all ancient terrorist groups that committed brutal murders. The number of Thuggees' victims alone is estimated to be as high as two million. These ancient terrorist groups in essence were religious groups—Jewish, Shi´ite and Kali worshippers. Much later, when the Crusaders conquered Jerusalem in 1099, they killed about 10,000 Muslims at Temple Mount and a huge number of Jews and Eastern Christians throughout Jerusalem. Modern times are no different. In 2016 alone, an estimated 1274 extreme Islamic terrorist attacks took place in fifty countries killing nearly 12,000 persons, injuring even more, and terrorizing communities and societies, at the very least making them anxious. The aim of this chapter is to study terrorism—especially terrorism linked to religion—from a psycho-historical perspective.

A BRIEF LOOK AT THE HISTORY OF TERRORISM

After the establishment of organized communities such as the first states of Sumer or Egypt more than 5,000 years ago, warfare turned one state against another state and one army against another army. On many occasions, the opposing armies were roughly of the same strength, and both sides utilized the same strategies and tactics. Nevertheless, nonconventional warfare, guerilla activities, and terrorism also took place. The term "guerrilla" comes from a Spanish word which means a "small war." Instead of being involved in major battles, the guerrillas split the war into many simultaneous or successive mini-wars. Terrorism, like guerrilla warfare, illustrates a significant imbalance in terms of opposing parties' power.

It is beyond the scope of this chapter to list practices of unconventional warfare throughout known history. I will reference the early twentieth century and Vladimir Ilyich Lenin's (1906) essay titled "Guerrilla Warfare," as it exemplifies a written justification and tactics of nonconventional warfare. Lenin stressed that Marxism "does not reject any form of struggle" (p. 213). Although he looked down on the nineteenth-century "Russian terrorists," Lenin suggested the same tactics: the aim was to assassinate individuals, chiefs and subordinates in the army and police, and to "confiscate monetary funds both from the government and from private persons" (p. 214). He demanded that "the worker combatant" (p. 216) should act under the strict control of the Social Democratic Labor Party. His aim for such killings of *selected* individuals was to achieve the point of an uprising. Then, "the uprising should assume the higher and more complex form of a prolonged civil war" (p. 216).

Lenin adopted concepts of nonconventional warfare from Karl Marx who had considered religion to be the opium of the people. Unlike today's extreme fundamentalist Islamic terrorists, Lenin and Marx were not asking their followers to act with a god's permission. Mao Zedong, taking what he learned from Lenin, described how a guerrilla swims among the people like a fish in the sea. We can see his views, in turn, directly reflected by Vo Nguyen Giap, the commander of Vietminh—League for the Independence of Vietnam—who sought independence for Vietnam from the French Empire. Giap´s "fish" were the villagers when it became very difficult for the enemy to differentiate between a fighter and a civilian. Therefore, the French tended to kill Vietnamese villagers en masse—guerrillas and innocents alike. A decisive defeat for the French at the battle of Dien Bien Phu in 1954 brought this armed conflict in Vietnam to an end (Suistola and Volkan, 2017).

The US involvement in the Vietnam War would peak later, but as early as June 6, 1962, during his speech at the United States Military Academy, President John F. Kennedy presented an accurate picture of the nature of the war his country was going to face: "We need to be prepared to fight a different war. This is another type of war, new in its intensity, ancient in its origin, war by guerrillas, subversives, insurgents, assassins; war by ambush instead of combat, by infiltration instead of aggression, seeking victory by eroding and exhausting the enemy instead of engaging him and these are the challenges that will be before us in the next decade if freedom is to be saved, a whole new kind of strategy, a wholly different kind of force, and therefore a new and wholly different kind of military training."

I will not list here the "different kinds of war" that were also taking place elsewhere, such as during the great wave of decolonization that started with the historical independence of India and Pakistan in 1947 and continued through Asia and Africa in the 1950s and 1960s. What is important to note is the big difference between the killing of others under the conditions described in Lenin's book and those carried out today by Al-Qaeda and the so-called Islamic State, ISIS. Today any innocent civilian can be a target of murderous acts for the sake of terrorizing the Other, and terrorists have "permission" to carry out their horrible deeds in the name of their God who would never negotiate with the Other's God to reach peaceful co-existence. The spread of suicide bombers and lone wolves also differentiates terrorism from the guerrillas of the Cuban Revolution who paved the way for another kind of nonconventional warfare we call "terrorism" and other earlier terrorists such as those in Northern Ireland. Like most historians, I do not consider what happened in Northern Ireland to have been a religious struggle between Catholics and Protestants. The IRA does not stand for "Catholic Army." The conflict in Northern Ireland, like the one on the Mediterranean island of Cyprus between Orthodox Christian Cypriot Greeks and Muslim Cypriot Turks, was a territorial conflict, not a religious one.

When Iran was in a desperate position at the early stages of the war between Iran and Iraq, which lasted from 1980 to 1988, the Supreme Leader Ayatollah Ruhollah Khomeini introduced a new weapon to terrorism—child suicide bombers—and initiated a culture of martyrdom. Earlier, toward the end of World War II, Japan systematically began using suicide pilots, so-called Kamikazes, although Kamikazes were not terrorists. The first child suicide bomber was thirteen-year-old Mohammed Hossein Fahmideh who destroyed a tank in a suicide attack. After him, thousands of children were recruited as suicide bombers (Caschetta, 2015). Later Hezbollah, a Shi'a Islamist militant group based in Lebanon and a terrorist organization, also used this new "weapon." Hezbollah's first suicide bombing attack took place in November 1982, and thereafter many terrorist organizations began using the same method. Suicide bombers are very efficient "weapons" for terrorism: as "weapons," they are cheap. There is no need to prepare an escape plan in a suicide bombing. Also, if it is successful, no informant will be left behind (Suistola and Volkan, 2017).

Although internationalization of terrorism in modern times began around 1970 with the Palestinian terrorist organizations, the September 11, 2001, attacks made it global, and fighting against terrorism also became global. I must add that, in a sense, all terrorist movements can be considered ideological, even when religion is "hijacked" (Thomson [with Aukofer], 2011) for violence. Nonreligious and religious ideological movements draw their fundamental principles from various sources and holy scriptures, be it *das Kapital* or the Bible or Koran.

MY BACKGROUND IN STUDYING INTERNATIONAL RELATIONSHIPS AND TERRORISM

I was born eighty-four years ago in Cyprus to Turkish parents, at a time when Cypriot Greeks and Cypriot Turks lived in peace, sometimes next door to each other. I came to the United States in 1957, eight months after graduating from Ankara School of Medicine in Turkey. By that time, Cypriot Greeks' investment in *Enosis,* union with Greece, had flared up. They were fighting, using terrorism, against the British on the island. The Cypriot Turks wanted *Taksim*, a "division" of the island between Cypriot Greeks and Cypriot Turks. Intercommunal violence between Cypriot Greeks and Cypriot Turks erupted a year before my arrival in the United States and lasted until the Republic of Cyprus was established in 1960 with an unworkable constitution that divided power between the Greek and Turkish communities. Within three years fresh violence began, and all the Cypriot Turks were forced to live in dreadful enclaves on only three percent of the island for eleven years. In 1974, the Turkish military from Turkey divided the island de facto into northern Turkish Cypriot and southern Greek Cypriot sections. The island still remains divided, while internationally (except for Turkey) only the Greek side's administered government is recognized as representing the Republic of Cyprus.

Just before my coming to the United States, during my last two years at the medical school and as a newly graduated physician, I had lived in a small apartment in Ankara, Turkey, with another medical student from Cyprus, Erol Mulla, who was like my younger brother. Several months after I arrived in the United States, Erol returned to Cyprus to visit his ailing mother. When he went to a pharmacy to buy some medicine for her, he was shot seven times, killed by a Cypriot Greek terrorist. I realized much later that this tragedy was the motivation for my getting involved in international relations and unofficial diplomacy when the opportunity presented itself in early 1980s. It also initiated my study of terrorism and complications of mourning.

As decades passed, while working away from my psychoanalytic couch with national, ethnic, or religious large groups, I began to consider the concept of large-group psychology in *its own right.* In the psychological literature, the term "large group" sometimes refers to 30–150 members who meet in a therapeutic setting in order to deal with a given psychological issue. This term is also sometimes associated with a large number of individuals coming together from opposing ethnic groups for exploring a special social/political conflict to gain insights and make individualized and communal attitudinal changes. My use of the term "large group" does not refer to members of such gatherings. It refers to tens, hundreds of thousands, or millions of individuals—most of whom will never meet during their lifetimes—who share sentiments, language, cultural amplifiers and historical "memories." Revising Erik Erikson's (1956) description of individual identity, I define *large-group identity*—whether it refers to ethnicity, nationality, religion, or ideology—as the subjective experience of thousands or millions of people. Large-group identities are articulated in terms of commonality such as: we are Basque; we are Lithuanian Jews; we are Polish; we are Sunni Muslims; we are capitalist.

Generally speaking, psychoanalysts have examined what a large group means for the individual. Freud (1921) described how the members of a large-group identify with each other and idealize and rally around their leader. Others (Anzieu, 1984; Chasseguet-Smirgel, 1984; Kernberg, 1980) wrote about fantasies shared by members of a large group. They suggested that large groups represent idealized mothers (breast mothers) who repair narcissistic injuries. It is assumed that external processes that threaten the group members' shared image of an idealized mother can initiate political processes and influence international affairs. But even so, these theories primarily focus on individuals' perceptions. They do not offer *specificity* concerning what exists within a special large group's psychology itself, what external event initiates it, and what may be useful in a diplomatic or political strategy to tame or prevent massive aggression.

Considering large-group psychology *in its own right* refers to making formulations as to conscious and unconscious shared psychological experiences and motivations of tens, hundreds of thousands, or millions of individuals' experiences and motivations that initiate specific social, cultural, political, ideological processes in the large group and modify its relationships with other large groups. Looking at large groups from this perspective is similar to the process psychoanalysts follow in their clinical practice when they make formulations about how they understand their analysands' internal worlds and their behavior patterns.

Analysts examine how analysands' developmental histories associated with various unconscious fantasies influence these individuals' personality organizations and symptom formations. When I was involved in unofficial diplomacy, such as conducting years-long dialogues between Soviets and Americans, Israelis and Egyptians/Palestinians, Estonian and Russians, Georgian and South Ossetians, I benefited from having a historian on my team. This person would inform us of the history of the large groups whose representatives we were working with and also about the history of their shared involvement in a specific activity or way of thinking. One of the main starting points of co-operation between some psychoanalysts and historians goes back to William Langer's (1957) Christmas address at the American Historical Association when he was its president. He declared that the next assignment for historians should be paying attention to depth psychology. James William Anderson and Jerome Winer (2003) wrote: "All of history is made by individuals, whether they are leaders, creative thinkers, or members of a grouping of people. As a body of thought that best illuminates the inner world, psychoanalysis has a natural relevance for the study of history. It can help get at the motivations of individuals and groups, it can offer possible explanations for many of history's mysteries, and it can also make sense of relationships between people" (p. 1). During our decades of work bringing representatives of "enemy" large groups for unofficial dialogues, a historian, Norman Itzkowitz, from Princeton University, was a member of our facilitating team. For a short time, Peter Loewenberg, a historian and a psychoanalyst from the University of California, also joined me in my international travels. In studying the present-day extreme Islamic religious fundamentalist terrorism, I worked with the Finnish historian, Jouni Suistola. In this chapter, my focus on Al-Qaeda and ISIS from a psycho-historical perspective is based on Suistola's and my joint studies (Suistola and Volkan, 2017).

LARGE-GROUP IDENTITY, CHOSEN TRAUMAS, AND CHOSEN GLORIES

Now I will go back to large-group identity for a closer look in order to clarify the main psychological motivation for Al-Qaeda and ISIS committing terrorism and suicide bombings. My experiences in international relationships has taught me that behind the observable reasons for conflicts between large groups or within a large group, such as political games or economic and legal issues, we find the psychology to protect and maintain large-group identity (Volkan, 1988, 1997, 2006, 2013, 2014). Religious terrorist organizations also perform their terrible acts to bring attention to and protect their type of large-group identity. Since they believe they have their God's approval it becomes harder to question why they become killers.

We can divide large-group identities into two types. The first type, as I stated above, refers to ethnic, religious, national, and political ideological investments *starting in childhood*. It exists throughout the world and is the end-result of myths and realities of common beginnings, historical continuities, geographical realities, and other shared linguistic, societal, religious, cultural, and historical factors. Elsewhere, I describe in detail how children develop their large-group identities through identifications with the adults around them and through being reservoirs of large-group-related elements that adults deposit in their developing self-representation. I also described how children learn about "shared targets," mostly inanimate things, from adults around them, and through them they learn *experientially* what belongs to their large group and what does not (Volkan, 1988, 2013, 2014). A good example of this concept can be found in Cyprus. As pork is part of the Greek diet, Greek farmers often raise pigs. While all children love farm animals, a Turkish child would be discouraged from touching a piglet, however adorable, as it would be perceived as "dirty" since Muslim Turks do not eat pork. Pigs do not belong in the Turk's large group, and for the Turkish child, the pig will be regarded as a cultural amplifier for the Greeks. In a concrete sense what is externalized into the image of the pig will not be reinternalized, will not be "eaten" psychologically.

Existing conditions in their environment direct children to invest in various types of large-group belonging. Indian psychoanalyst, Sudhir Kakar (1996), wrote that a child born in Hyderabad, India, would focus on religious/cultural issues as he or she develops a large-group identity, since adults there define their dominant large-group identity according to religious affiliation—Muslim or Hindu. In Cyprus, the developing child's main investment will be in nationality: he or she will be a Turk or a Greek.

To visualize the large-group identity that develops in childhood, in my previous writings, I imagined that we learn to wear two layers, like fabric, from the time we are children (Volkan, 1988, 2004, 2006). The first layer, the individual layer, fits each of us snugly, like clothing. It is one's *core* personal identity that provides an inner sense of "persistent sameness" (Erikson, 1956) for the individual. The second layer is like the canvas of a tent, which is loose fitting, but allows us to share a sense of sameness with others under the same large-group tent. While it is the tent pole—the political leader—that holds the tent erect, the tent's canvas psychologically protects both the leader and the group and represents the large-group identity that is shared by thousands or millions of people. On each tent canvas there are "identity markers" that only belong to the large group's members. On occasion, a design on a canvas, such as a certain religious symbol, may appear similar to a design on another huge tent's canvas. However, even under these circumstances we note "minor differences" in such elements. When conflicts arise between the two large groups, such minor differences become major concerns.

The shared mental images of the large group's real and fantasized, and/or mythologized, *historical* events are the most significant of identity markers. Such past events can be categorized as glorified or traumatic, what I call "chosen glories," and "chosen traumas" (Volkan, 1991). Shared mental images of pride- and pleasure-evoking past events and heroes are chosen glories, and they are recollected ritualistically. Chosen traumas are the shared mental images of an event in a large group's history wherein the group suffered a catastrophic loss, humiliation, and helplessness at the hands of enemies. This includes an inability to mourn. Sometimes chosen traumas and chosen glories appear intertwined.

In peaceful times, in a societal setting, chosen glories and chosen traumas remain dormant or recalled ritualistically, sometimes with ceremonies and holidays, but without major shared impact on the large group to which they belong. They are reactivated in order to temporarily heighten a people's shared sense of pride in their large group. Elsewhere I examined how, under changing historical times, the reactivation of chosen glories and chosen traumas by political leaders in order to increase shared large-group narcissism can lead to deadly new massive traumas. For example, after the collapse of the former Yugoslavia, Slobodan Milošević and people around him reactivated a six-hundred-year-old Serbian chosen trauma, the shared image of the Battle of Kosovo, in order to revitalize the Serbian large-group identity. It created a massive trauma for Bosnian Muslims (Volkan, 1996).

Membership in the second type of large-group identity takes place when individuals *are adults*. Business leaders' and employees' intense investment in big-business organizations, national or international, or many people joining the same professional organization, sports club, or political party can be imagined as belonging to the second type of large group. However, members of these kinds of groups do not lose their first type of large-group identity that was established in childhood. Terrorist organizations, such as Al-Qaeda and ISIS, truly illustrate the formation of the second type of large group. Members of such organizations, or lone wolves connected to them, function under the dominant impact of this second-type large-group identity. They lose their individual identities' influence—such as their personal moral codes—on their behavior patterns. Terrorists or suicide bombers carry out their inhumane acts not simply because of problems their individual identities started to develop in childhood, but primarily because psychologically, they become representatives of their adulthood's large group and perceive their horrific acts as their moral duty to protect or bring attention to their second-type large-group identity. Those in the second type of large terrorist groups are also intensely involved in grasping the chosen traumas and chosen glories in order to define, maintain, and protect their large-group identities.

GREEN BELT MOVEMENT: FOCUS ON A CHOSEN TRAUMA AND SEARCH FOR A "CALIPH"

The creation of the State of Israel and the US interventions in Iraq and Afghanistan have been openly examined for decades by the media and academicians as shameful and are humiliating events for a huge number of Arabs and Muslims elsewhere. Here, I will focus on rather "hidden" aspects of history and their psychological impacts in expanding extreme Islamic fundamentalism and the evolution of Al-Qaeda and ISIS.

First I will go back to 1979, when the Soviet Union occupied Afghanistan. This triggered a strengthening insurgence that attracted radicalized Muslims from Arab countries to join the fight against the Soviet infidels. Parallel to this movement were US efforts to construct a barrier to the Soviet Union along the Soviet's southern flank. A strategy developed in the United States that was usually known as the Green Belt strategy, the color green symbolizing Islam. Countries between Greece and China are Muslim, and the Green Belt idea aimed at increasing investment in Islam in these countries. By doing so, those who imagined and implemented this strategy hoped that Islam within the Soviet Union would also be inflamed and eventually target and undermine the Soviet Empire itself. Islamic schools (*madrassas*) for children and youth are not a new phenomenon in the Middle East or in other Muslim countries such as Pakistan. Although they have existed since the beginning of Islam, the Green Belt strategy greatly increased their number in Pakistan. What was different about these new Pakistani madrassas, funded by the United States as well as Great Britain and Saudi Arabia, was their inclusion of training in the service of future violence. The Saudis provided funding for the expansion of Wahhabism, and the teaching in these *madrassas* was influenced by Wahhabi as well as Deobandi versions of extreme religious "ideology" (Rashid, 2000). Deobandi comes from the name of a city in India about 150 kilometers from Delhi, Deoband, where the movement started in 1867 after a failed revolt against British rule.

For years, the children in the madrassas had been required to read the Quran in Arabic, a language they did not know, and so they had accepted the "interpretation" given to them by their teachers. When they read in Urdu, they were told that the Urdu letter *jeem* stood for jihad; *kaaf* for Kalashnikov, and *khy* for khoon (blood) (Ali, 2001). The "graduates" of these madrassas would later help constitute the foundation on which the Taliban and Al-Qaeda could stand.

During the 1980s, the number of foreign fighters known as Afghan Arabs rose to about 25,000. The Saudis and Americans financed the *mujahedeens*, a term used for Muslim fighters defending their religion. In addition, the Pakistani Inter-Services Intelligence trained about 80,000 fighters, and the Americans armed them. These sources provided a daunting mix of battle-hardened fighters, motivated by a radical interpretation of Islam. In 1989, at the close of the war with the Soviets, they strategized the battles ahead. The choice was terrorism. During the first half of the 1990s, the *mujahedeens'* enemies were mainly corrupt governments and authoritarian rulers in the Middle East.

While all this was taking place, and even earlier, there were attempts to rejuvenate the chosen glories of Islam. There were multiple events that can be considered starting points. One of them was the establishment, in the mid-1960s, of Dar al Tabligh al Islami (The Institute for the Propagation of Islam) in Shiite Iran, not an Arabic country. In 1990, historian Bernard Lewis noted: "Islamic fundamentalism has given an aim and a form to the otherwise aimless and formless resentment and anger of the Muslim masses at the forces that have devalued their traditional values and loyalties and, in the final analysis, robbed them of their beliefs, their aspirations, their dignity, and to an increasing extent even their livelihood" (p. 59). The United States ambassador to Kuwait during the Iraqi invasion of that country, Nathaniel Howell, referred to what was happening in the Arab world as the "nostalgia movement" (1997).

Here, I will focus on the role of one chosen trauma that Al-Qaida and then ISIS wanted to turn into a chosen glory. During the reign of Sultan Selim I (1512 to 1520), the Ottoman Turks took over Syria and Egypt, and by 1517, the Arab Sunni Caliphates had come to an end. The Ottoman Sultan assumed the title and inherited the role of defender of the holiest places in Islam—the very cradle of Islam—the cities of Mecca and Medina. The Ottoman Sultan's double role as religious leader (Caliph) and political defender of the Islamic world lasted until the end of the Ottoman Empire and until, rising from the Empire's ashes, the secular Turkish Republic was established in 1923. With the birth of modern Turkey, the Caliphate—in a sense, Sunni Islam's "papacy"—was abolished, and centuries of Islam's established leadership suddenly disappeared. The Ottoman Empire, the former defender of Islam, was in tatters, and Turks were busy establishing a new large-group identity in the face of its so-called "Westernization" struggles. Meanwhile, the Arabs and many other Muslims remained helplessly exposed to greater influence and manipulation by Western powers.

Elie Kedourie (1970) reports details of the British government's disastrous handling of the Middle East after the collapse of the Ottoman Empire and its humiliation of the Arabs and other Muslims. Even before the Caliphate was abolished, the British would alternately raise and dash expectations for establishing a caliphate outside of the Ottoman territory. They claimed to support establishing the Caliphate in either India or an Arab country, thereby creating tension and division between Indian and Arab Muslims.

A man psychologically searching for a stable father figure re-inflamed the "hidden" chosen trauma—when Others humiliated Arabs and other Muslims—by playing political games: promising the honor to name a Caliph from one of their large groups but never doing so. Problems within this man's own internal would be intertwined with large-group processes.

A psychoanalyst has to be very careful in writing a psychobiography of an individual who has never been on his or her couch. However, there were enough data for Peter Olsson (2008) and I (2004), each of us working independently, to examine the psychological reasons for Osama bin Laden's search for a stable father figure (a Caliph). Very briefly, Osama bin Laden's mother, originally from Syria, was "exiled" from his father's harem when he was one-year-old, leaving him in the care of his "stepmothers" who called him *Iban al Abeda* (son of the slave). This was certainly a factor in why he developed a revengeful character. All indications are that his father, with 54 children, did not have much time for him. Osama's father died in a plane crash when Osama was 10 years old, and his older brother Salem, who could have been a father or big-brother figure for Osama, was also killed in an air tragedy—this time, a helicopter accident. He frantically searched for a father figure, psychologically speaking, to pull him from an environment of "bad" mother figures in order to reach up on his psychological developmental ladder. I must add here that if Osama bin Laden had not inherited an estimated 80 million dollars after his father's death, he might have remained harmless and would not have been involved with Al-Qaeda.

Al-Qaeda searched for the Caliphate. ISIS established the so-called Islamic State and declared the Caliphate in June 2014, and the appointment of Caliph Ibrahim took place. His name was originally Ibrahim al-Awwad and then Abu Bakr al-Baghdadi. Caliph Ibrahim is introduced as a member of al-Qurashi, Prophet Mohammed´s tribe, which would legitimize him as a Caliph. The Caliphate's future "action program" was also summarized in the declaration: construction of state institutions with governors, Sharia courts, an educational system based on *madrassas*, taxation, as well as demolition of "crosses and graves" and "removing of devil."

Although I had plenty of information about Osama bin Laden's life (Volkan, 2004), I have very little information about Abu Bakr al-Baghdadi's life history. I know some facts, such as his claim that he received a PhD from the Islamic University of Baghdad. He keeps a low profile. This reminds me of the Muslim custom of not painting human figures, not looking at a drawing of Mohammad. There is a possibility that the lack of pictures of al-Baghdadi in social media makes him an even stronger and more holy figure for his diaspora followers—this and ISIS' efforts to show how important glory is in motivating people to join ISIS, especially young persons, searching for a "container" for their psychological being (Suistola and Volkan, 2017).

I coined the term "time collapse" to denote the conscious and unconscious connections between a large group's past historical trauma and contemporary threats that typically emerge when a chosen trauma is drastically reactivated (Volkan, 1991, 1997). The reactivation of shared anxieties, expectations, fantasies, and defenses associated with the chosen trauma magnifies the image of the current enemies and current conflicts. Time collapse may lead to irrational and sadistic or masochistic decision-making by the leadership of a large group; in turn, members of the large group may become psychologically prepared for sadistic or masochistic acts, and, in the worst-case scenario, perpetrate monstrous cruelty against others

We can observe "time collapse" in the ISIS' activities. The position of ISIS can be compared to the first 25 years of the history of Islam: victory over superior enemies and rapid expansion. Also, the Caliphate includes Muslims everywhere, not only those in the Islamic State. But, both Al-Qaida and ISIS encouraged and used suicide bombers, a new type of weapon.

Suicide Bombers

On September 15, 1982, Israeli Defense Forces circled two adjacent Palestinian refugee camps, Sabra and Shatila, in West Beirut. In the late afternoon of the following day, the Lebanese Christian Phalangist militia, allies of the Israelis, attacked the camps, indiscriminately killing civilians trapped in the cramped streets. In 1991, I met five children survivors in Tunisia at a Palestinian orphanage called Beit Atfal Assumoud (the Home of Children of Steadfastness). At that time, the headquarters of the Palestinian Liberation Organization (PLO) was located in Tunis, and the PLO administered the orphanage. All five survivors were infants when the attack on the Sabra and Shatila camps occurred. Since their real identities were unknown, they were all given the last name "Arafat," after the PLO chairman who was a frequent visitor to the orphanage.

For a week I examined the five Sabra and Shatila children (and other orphans living there). When I first saw them playing together, they appeared as "normal" children do in play. However, I also observed that they would remain together as a "team," and if one of them were separated from the others, he or she would become agitated. On the fifth day of my visit to the orphanage, I attempted to interview these children one by one, with the aid of an interpreter. All of them then became "abnormal"—one hallucinated, and another literally destroyed the interview room. As soon as they were placed together again, as a "team," they appeared to be "normal" once more. I concluded that they must have difficulties in their sense of personal identity; on the other hand, as a team they each appeared "normal." This observation taught me a lot about replacing, to one extent or another, a person's individual identity with a "team" identity.

This situation reminded me of another historical period when intentional interference with the personal identities of children occurred—when the "cracks" in German children's personal identities were filled with Nazi ideology. Official guidance, as presented in Nazi physician, Joanna Haarer's, books (Haarer, 1937, 1943) (see also Volkan, Ast, and Greer 2002), counseled parents to feed their children only on a rigorous schedule and not to rush to their children when they cried or encountered trouble in their surroundings. Mothers of the Nazi period were directed to ignore their children's natural dependency needs, and thus they ruined the children's sense of basic trust. Children were forced to experience the sense that there was no benevolent power in their surroundings and were robbed of the opportunity to identify with a nurturing parent. Further, frustrated by their parents' behavior, children projected their own angry feelings onto their parents, imagining their elders to be more aggressive than they might have actually been in reality. In turn, they felt that the only way to protect themselves was to become aggressors, "tough" kids. This interference with personal identity formation was connected to Nazi propaganda. Children's "cracks" in personal identity formation were directly or indirectly filled with Nazi propaganda so that as adults these children would be "tough" and experience no feelings of remorse for destroying "undesirables" like Jews.

This work in Tunisia and my reading about Nazi era children in Germany started me thinking about how suicide bombers replace their personal identities with their second-type large-group identity. Some years after visiting Tunisia, I began collecting information on how the Islamic fundamentalist suicide bombers in the Middle East were trained (Volkan, 1997). When I was an Inaugural Yitzhak Rabin Fellow in Israel in late 2000 and early 2001, I received more information on this topic; however, I never myself interviewed a Palestinian suicide bomber who had survived.

Most future suicide bombers were chosen as teenagers. Their education was carried out in small groups. These groups collectively read the Quran and chanted religious scriptures. Unlike most of the Pakistani and Afghan "students" in Pakistani madrassas, the Palestinian "students" were able to understand what they were reading in the Arabic Quran. For this reason, their readings were carefully selected. For example, they would read how, during the Battle of Badr (624 CE), Prophet Muhammad told his followers they would continue to "live" in Paradise if they died during the battle. The "teachers" also would supply sacred-sounding, but meaningless, phrases to be repeated over and over in chant, such as "I will be patient until patience is worn out from patience." Meanwhile, suicide bomber candidates were instructed not to inform their parents of their missions. The "teachers" also forbid things such as music and television on the grounds that they could be sexually stimulating. Sex and women could be obtained only after a passage to adulthood. However, the "passage" was killing oneself, and it was not called "suicide." The youngsters were told that life continues in Paradise. The oedipal triumph was allowed after this passage by the satisfaction of libidinal wishes by *houris* (angels) in Paradise.

The future suicide bomber would become an agent of the large-group identity and would attempt to repair it for him- or herself and for other members of the large group. Killing one's self (and one's personal identity) and Others would not matter. What mattered would be that the act of terrorism would bring self-esteem and attention to the large-group identity. While I was in Israel, I learned that the death of a suicide bomber was celebrated as a "wedding ceremony." However, this was given up when there was a negative response to it by the Palestinians themselves.

After the September 11 attacks, people began talking about "a new breed" of Islamic extreme fundamentalist suicide terrorists. Before, most were young Palestinians who had been humiliated directly or indirectly personally or were relatives or friends of those who had been. These new terrorists were mostly from Egypt and Saudi Arabia, older and from wealthy, educated families. By all appearances, these were indeed a new breed of terrorist. However, closer scrutiny reveals that the psychological mechanisms that create standard Islamic fundamentalist suicide bombers applied to this new group of terrorists as well.

Let us return to a metaphoric tent covering a large group with its canvas representing this large group's identity. The more this canvas shakes and is perceived to be unstable—not only due to the Other's humiliating attacks but also due to local circumstances—the more individuals are attracted, even if they are rich and educated, to wearing the tent's canvas as their primary garment and trying to stabilize its shaking.

I have no direct data about ISIS training future suicide bombers. However, there is a paper reporting interviews with ISIS defectors (Speckhard and Yayla, 2015). According to these defectors, ISIS also has very young boys in their training camps with the intention that they become suicide bombers in the future. Also, according to these defectors, the future suicide bombers' "graduation ceremonies" require a graduate to execute one of the enemy prisoners who are housed for this purpose near the training camp. Meanwhile there is information that some suicide bombers had joined the terrorist organization only a few weeks before they were called upon to attack (Berman, 2009).

Terrorism and the "Who Are We Now" Civilization

Terroristic attacks at many locations of the world have played and are playing a significant role in the development of what I call the "Who are We Now?" civilization. First, let me explain what I mean by this metaphorical question. In the second half of the twentieth century, especially in the 1950s and 1960s, in order to explain changes in nations, Modernization Theory, as expounded by sociologist Talcott Parsons (1967), gained prominence. It was expected that (1) industry and trade would replace agriculture in the economy; 2) industrial society would require universal values that would replace tribal and local values; and (3) new forms of communication would lead to cultural assimilation. Modernization expressed in urbanization, industrialization, together with the development of education and communications systems, would destroy ethnic identities as ethnic groups became assimilated into larger societies (Harle, 2000). Just the reverse has happened, as ethnic identities have gathered new strength in the face of various levels of dehumanization engendered by modernization. In many ways, the fate of Modernization Theory is similar to that of the Leninist notion that the classless society ushered in by socialism would form a bulwark against wars that were the ultimate product of capitalist society. The unfolding of history undermined both Modernization Theory and the notion of a peaceful, classless society. Despite efforts to bury ethnicity, it is still here and most likely will continue to be with us into the foreseeable future.

Change in the twenty-first century is occurring at an unprecedented pace and scale. Globalization, incredible advances in communication and travel technologies have made people with different large-group identities interact more and more and faster and faster. Such developments, alongside their positive aspects, have brought confrontations and conflicts among religious, ethnic, national, or ideological large groups. The idea of having an ethnically pure national identity or being a "synthetic nation" like the United States (Loewenberg, 1995), but composed of only *selected* people from *selected* locations is an illusion in our present-day world. Furthermore, Europe is in the midst of a refugee crisis, as are many other locations filled with refugees. In many places, the refugee issue is now and then linked to terrorism. Large numbers of people in host countries are busy with realistic and fantasized fears, trying to define their large-group identities (Volkan, 2017).

Recent historical events such as Brexit and Donald Trump's winning the presidential election in the United States in 2016 are linked to such societal/psychological conditions. Many people in England now seem to believe something like this: "We can choose newcomers to our country, such as people from Canada, but the unwanted Others from undesirable locations cannot disturb our glorious large-group identity." On many occasions, Donald Trump has mentioned the importance of protecting the "American identity" and has expressed his appreciation of Great Britain's efforts, through Brexit, to hold on to its large-group identity. During the presidential election, Trump even called himself "Mr. Brexit." Trump's "wall" between the United States and Mexico, accompanied by his remarks indicating his desire to keep Muslims out of the United States, became a symbol of a protective psychological border of large-group identity for a huge number of persons in the United States.

It can be stated that we now live in what I call a "Who are we now?" civilization that is accompanied by terror and anxiety. In large-group histories, we see the appearance of this metaphorical question following historical events such as war, revolution, a humiliating economic trauma, the coming to power of or loss of a charismatic reparative or destructive leader. The colonialists leaving Africa and the collapse of the Soviet Union and former Yugoslavia were significant earlier historical events in the development of this new civilization.

What is new in our present world is the spreading globally of the question "Who are we now?" Without being aware of its hidden psychological influence, many present-day political leaders have become involved in finding answers to this question, usually going back and re-activating chosen traumas, chosen glories, and old cultural amplifiers in one way or another. In China, for example, there is an intense investment in a chosen glory. In 2014, three new national holidays were introduced to celebrate China's victory over Japan (*The Economist*, November 19–25, 2016, p. 53). The globalization of "Who are we now?" often manifests as a return to extreme right-wing conservatism. In some European countries parties, such as Viktor Orban's party Fidesz (Hungarian Civic Alliance) in Hungary and Jaroslaw Kaczynski's Law and Justice Party in Poland, have even taken leadership roles in politics. Marine Le Pen's National Front in France and Geert Wilders' Party for Freedom in Holland are also influential. What these political parties have in common is not only exaggerated nationalism but also xenophobia, such as in the case of Party for Freedom that has a strong anti-Islamic flavor. Meanwhile, the president of Turkey, Tayyip Erdoğan, and his ruling political party, are attempting to return to the Ottoman religious and cultural customs. This is causing a serious division within the Turkish society.

Utilizing chosen traumas and chosen glories for increasing large-group narcissism and conservatism is not dangerous by itself. But its exaggeration and contamination with malignant prejudice against the Other, or racism, certainly creates severe problems. We have such problems in our present world. All these lead to divisions or fragmentation within many countries' populations. Let us not forget that Al-Qaeda and ISIS, searching for revenge for old chosen traumas and nostalgia for old chosen glories, are busy with the "Who are we now?" question. Their hateful terroristic activities are linked to refugees. This supports the maintenance of the worldwide "who are we now situation" and political changes in many countries, including the United States.

CONCLUDING REMARKS

Imagine a murky lake full of dangerous alligators. Counterterrorist activities primarily aim to rid the world of alligators that leave the lake, move onto the land, and eat people. The real point of this analogy is to understand what exists in this lake that feeds these dangerous reptiles in the first place and helps them to multiply. Having said this, I admit that psycho-historical knowledge does not give us a specific tool to abolish terrorism. It may, however, be helpful in developing more sophisticated counterterrorism strategies. In reality, I think that at the present time, the gap between the United States and others' aim to destroy ISIS and the terrorist organization's aim to establish a global caliphate is simply astronomical.

Chapter 5

The Roles of Essentialism and Religion as Scaffolds to Terrorism

Some Psycho-historical Considerations

Vincenzo Sanguineti

Philosopher and social theorist, Kwame Anthony Appiah (2015), British-born by parents from Ghana and the United States, defines essentialism as the universal need for human groups to have strong core properties in common (properties that would make all their members essentially the same), and as the universal inclination for humans to attribute deep commonalities (in physical, geographical, religious ways) to alike-looking people (people who look alike are also intrinsically alike and share essentially the same value systems). The essentialist view considers factors such as gender, sexuality, race, ethnicity, or other group characteristics as fixed traits, discounting variation among group members as secondary. Essentialism, therefore, is the primary component of the boundary between the "we" and the "they." When conceptualized from this perspective, essentialism assumes the qualities of a powerful collective organizing template for social relatedness and behavior. Professor of psychology and cognitive science at Yale University, Paul Bloom (2010), has stated that:

> One of the most exciting ideas in cognitive science is the theory that people have a default assumption that things, people and events have invisible essences that make them what they are. Experimental psychologists have argued that essentialism underlies our understanding of the physical and social worlds, and developmental and cross-cultural psychologists have proposed that it is instinctive and universal. We are natural-born essentialists (p. 3)

One can plausibly envision the concept as a prototype for group identity, with roots reaching as far in the past as to the first tribes of the genus Homo, and perhaps even further back, to the earliest organized groups of pre-hominids and of their evolutionary ancestors. It clarified and specified tribal characteristics and membership and it marked tribal-specific totems, as well as specific taboos and purification rituals. Examples of group cohesion and differentiation between the "we" and the "they" have also been described within the nonhuman natural world, among primates, for instance (Cheney and Seaforth, 2007).

The aspiration to essentialism is heightened whenever the psyche is subjected to a major migration, the term describing, in a psychological sense, a major and enduring shift in the sociocultural landscape of the subject. Whoever migrates across the complex boundaries dividing large systems that differ in their languages, in their social structures, and in their traditions, is caught between a feeling of estrangement or alienation, and a feeling of assimilation or belonging. The estrangement is due to the persistence of some degree of variance, of not complete alignment, between the new landscape and what was experienced and then left behind on the other side of the boundary. To that side belonged all the experiences of the individual's early formative years of development, which carried essentialist messages and played significant roles in early psychic organization. As an example, concerning language, Nick Mansfield, professor in Critical and Cultural Studies at Macquarie University, states that: "Anyone who has experienced the liminal space where one language meets another is aware of the untranslatable dimension that divides one symbolic order from another" (cited in Sanguineti, 2007, p. XIV).

Assimilation stems out of the desire to belong, to become not-different, and to become fully "mixed with the crowd"; in other words, to recreate the original protective feeling of group essentialism that dissipated during the process of migration.

In his paper, "Gods do not negotiate: a psycho-historical look at terrorism" Professor Vamik Volkan outlined the historical development of systems that focused on the vengeful repudiation and destruction of established orders, and became a banner, a symbolic tent, under which the individual wounded and lost psyche could seek an answer to its urgent aspiration toward a renewed essentialism, enhanced by its present condition of alienation. In the case of terroristic indoctrination, this pressing need for a strong group identity is magnified by the evocation from the doctrine leaders of specific and shared sets of severe narcissistic wounds or inflated narcissistic objectives (conditions that Volkan labels "chosen traumas" and "chosen glories"); and by the complete erosion of trust toward the Other (in many cases enhanced by the malignant propaganda of the leaders). A passionate, total mistrust of the Other, impermeable to alternative suggestions, is often found at the foundations of extreme movements.

This emotion of mistrust is born out of a feeling of profound betrayal by an originally looked-for and deeply trusted protective system that abandoned its commitment to the subject because of ideological contamination and corrupting greed; it equals loss of previously felt trust. Its dynamics recall the specific sets of dynamics that in the individual psyche eventually come to dictate the relationship between the Subject and the (parental, significant) Other along affective lines. This process is explored at depth in the first stage of trust versus mistrust of Erikson's (1950) theory of psychosocial development. Mistrust needs to be differentiated from the similar but dynamically different state of distrust for a different ideology with opposing values to which the individual, separated by his own essentialism, has never belonged. Distrust is a common condition in political systems: *among* nations as well as *within* a nation, where it is commonly expressed as party division, and can become highly polarizing.[1]

A source of crucial energy common to most terroristic movements derives from a religious-ideological migration of some sort and eventuates in intense religious fanaticism: the term migration applies in that religious fanaticism often emerges from an initial conflict with, and disconnectedness from, the larger system of the moderate religious majority that failed to recognize, protect, and nurture; the defrauded, marginalized fanatic claims then to be the true representative of the pure, uncontaminated form of his religion, and describes himself as the faithful soldier at the service of a God that has been betrayed by the corrupted majority through compromises and negotiations.

In the case of terrorism, the "god theme" has become a very effective weapon in the hands of the leaders, who exploit an implied or direct link to the God as a way to promote and continue their personal agenda. The distorted use of the divine in the teaching of children, both in the Pakistani and Lebanese madrassas, and of which Volkan gives several highly disturbing examples in his paper, is a very impressive example of religion being "hijacked" for political reasons—in this case extreme violence. It illustrates how "religious fervor"—true or false—is used by organizations as Al Qaeda and ISIS for recruitment, training, and sustained provision of an ongoing motivation to self-sacrifice.

This particular and stunning misuse of God's message and meaning calls for a search of the factors, during the psycho-historical development of the divine and of the gods themselves, which would shed light on how such distorted religious fervor happened to unfold within the human psyche. The consolidation of temporal and secular powers upon a single person has been a basic instrument for rulers since the dawn of history, probably on a planetary scale. For the power hungry, state and church have always worked particularly well together. The chief-priest and the sovereign-god images were sought for, accepted and revered concepts throughout ancient Western history, as with—among many others—the Egyptian Pharaohs, the Persian kings, and the Hittite and the Roman emperors. Leaders gifted with divine attributes offered to their constituencies a substantially greater degree of reliability, trustworthiness, and protective ability than mere mortals could.

It is therefore not surprising that the distortion and misappropriation of the divine message perpetrated in the madrassas, which counted on the trustfulness, naiveté, and faith of their young subjects, evokes the memory of a similar event from a very distant past, equally outlandish but quite different in its outcome. Herodotus reports how, around 559 BCE, the tyrant Pisistratus planned to reestablish his lost tyranny in Athens, from which he had been exiled three years before. He was considered to be an extreme advocate of the people—mostly the poor, the downtrodden, and the forsaken—and he badly needed to rouse again his party base: Athens was then a direct democracy and the popular vote was the decisive political factor (much sorely missed this option during the last US Presidential election). Pisistratus found a tall and beautiful woman, possibly a flower-girl called Phye, from a different region, dressed her to look like the goddess of the city Athena, and drove her in his chariot into the city, preceded by heralds loudly declaring that the Athenians should receive back Pisistratus because the very goddess was bringing him back from exile to her own acropolis. Although the Athenians, as Herodotus does not fail to point out, were the most intelligent among the Greeks, still Pisistratus' party base apparently fell for the ruse; they flooded the streets, received the couple with acts of reverence, and installed him back as tyrant of the city. The collective psyche of the party needed desperately to believe that their voices were listened to. The lie was admirably tuned to satisfy that need, by offering the mirage of special divine support: the very goddess of the city, fully personified!

These instances, spanning from a large group of dispossessed and resentful citizens two and a half millennia ago to the radicalization and exploitation of the present-day child suicide bombers, share the extent of the seductive power contained in the specific delusional belief of achieving special attention from the God. Pisistratus' party and the ISIS fanatics differ profoundly, however, in what was perceived as the will of the God. Some profound psycho-historical change did indeed happen, through these two and a half millennia: a substantial transformation in the perception of the spiritual realm with its system of values and ethics that allowed for the conception, the gestation, the emergence within the human psyche of such a horrific, cruel, vengeful, and unbending God, and the widespread acceptance of such an extreme dark conceptualization of the transcendent as a fully veritable reality.

The switch from polytheism to monotheism represented a radical change in the psychohistory of the religious metaphor, through which the collective and individual psyche of humanity has tried, probably since its origin, to capture and clarify the meaning and the expression of its relationship to the universally perceived realms of the supernatural or transcendental; indeed, anthropologist Clifford Geertz (1993) has referred to religion as to how humanity relates to a cosmic "order of existence."

The ancient polytheistic religions had imbedded in their polyhedral, multifaceted structure some interesting and moderating elements. Old records describe a widespread recognition that all cultures share and worship the same gods, although under different names and by different rituals. So, the Greek "Athena" was also the "Maliya" of the Hittites and the "Neth" of the Egyptians, their altars being interchangeable in the offering of prayers and reverence; "Zeus" was also "Tarhunt" among the Hittites and "Ammon" in Egypt, while "Aphrodite" was "Padritahi" and "Hathon," and so on. Monotheism forcefully dictated the repudiation of the false gods and persecuted them, opening the door to the concept of expelling from the congregation of some chosen ones (the like to a symbolic tent of professor Volkan), all the undesirables, using all possible means: from the terror of the Inquisition to the terror of the suicide bomber. The Inquisition was certainly a sophisticated tool for sadistic terror: one never knew when the "witches hammer" would fall, and the terror from its refined methods of torture and the auto-da-fe' or burning at the stake, to which people were obligated to attend, or risk to be accused of heresy, would certainly surpass the present anxious expectations from the next terrorist attack. In these contexts the false believer, deprived of the soul-symbol, is degraded to a nonhuman condition. Once such a scenario is set, a violent patriarchy, preaching the will of an exclusive, and violent, patriarchal deity, can easily attain the extreme of terrorism in response to real or imagined traumata and needs.

In those ancient polytheistic pantheons, the individual and collective human psyche developed while surrounded by a multiplicity of powerful goddesses, at times dangerous and to be feared, but mainly representative of very important functions, such as crafts, wisdom, justice, love, fecundity, maternity, birth, marriage, and even war. They represented ever-present and acknowledged internalized aspects of the psyche: a psychological matriarchy able to exercise an important complementing effect on the masculine counterpart. The largely or exclusively patriarchal structure of the contemporary monotheistic religions has no space anymore for those matriarchal components. One is left to speculate why the roles listed above appear to have been removed from the shelf of the divine (a most dramatic visual representation of this erasure of the feminine is the burqa: the feminine is forcefully hidden from view, forced under a cover that imposes anonymity and reduces womanly characteristics to an undifferentiated black nonentity, along the format psychologically as well as physically decided and designed by the patriarchy). Uncontested male-driven templates may then become so inflated within the psyche to eventuate in self-justified, narcissistic "Arcs Unbound" conditions. This term was used to connote the fully unrestrained and destructive conflagration of the war-god Ares: a state similar to the condition that Jung (1936) considered for Hitler, whom he saw as the personified archetype of the German war god, Wotan.

The Homeric pantheon represented a second generation of deities; the collective psyche of the time had moved forward from the earliest, inhuman monstrous figures of the supernatural realm, highly destructive forces largely residing in the subterranean depth of nature (and of the psyche), and it articulated the highly human family of the Olympian gods. This new generation of Greek deities decried senseless bloodshed and cruelty, and was quite reluctant to being pulled into fighting. The battle of the gods in Book XXI of Homer's (circa 900BC) *The Iliad* is a very watered down, almost perfunctory confrontation, in comparison with the human counterpart that goes on around them, and it ends rather quickly in negotiated retreats and compromises. While *The Iliad* describes repeatedly how the gods could inspire abject terror, they did so primarily by psychological means rather than by horrific killings. Zeus has a special tool, the aegis, which he lends to other gods—the chosen ones being Apollo and Athena—to shake in front of the armies in order to spread terror and send in flight either the Greeks or the Trojans, and in that way keep the war balanced.

All these images suggest profound differences in the perception of the god-symbols between the ancient polytheistic systems and the more recent monotheistic ones. It appears as if the reorganization of the realm of the spirit into an exclusively patriarchal domain has also opened the door to the conceptualization of diminished male gods, captured inside very distinct tents—to use once more Professor Vulcan's apt symbolism—and vested with reciprocal animosity if not full hatred. The images suggest a psycho-historical progression (or regression?) along the Freudian concept of the monotheistic God as being an adaptation of the father image, and religious belief as being at bottom infantile and neurotic. The contamination of the religious metaphor by patriarchal aggression finds an echo in Freud's (1912–1913) application to religion, "Totem and Taboo," of the theme of the Oedipus complex and in his mentioning that a patricidal ceremony was the beginning of so many things—of societal organization, of moralistic restrictions, and religion.[2]

Psychology has dedicated significant attention to the pervasive phenomenon of religion—or spirituality, or transcendence, or supernatural, among the various metaphors—seeking an understanding of its sources and meanings. During the past century alone, several scholars, aside from Freud, have advanced their interpretations of this universal individual and collective manifestation of the psyche. Among these, William James (1902) came to be considered the founder of the psychological study of religion with his work, *The Varieties of Religious Experience: A Study in Human Nature*. In it, James collected a series of lectures delivered at the University of Edinburgh in Scotland in 1901 and 1902. The lectures concerned the nature of religion and the neglect of science in the academic study of religion. In them, he expressed his interest in direct religious experience rather than in institutional religion: "I speak not now of your ordinary religious believer, who follows the conventional observances of his country, whether it be Buddhist, Christian, or Mohammedan. His religion has been made for him by others, communicated to him by tradition, determined to fixed forms by imitation, and retained by habit. It would profit us little to study this second-hand religious life. We must make search rather for the original experiences which were the pattern-setters to all this mass of suggested feeling and imitated conduct" (p. 13). Also, and pertinent to the present topic, James believed that the origins of a religion shed little light upon its value. There is a distinction between an existential judgment (on constitution, origin, and history) and a proposition of value (a judgment on importance, meaning, or significance).

Many of these scholarly studies addressed the monotheistic metaphor of the divinity: the patriarchal "God," a single entity (masculine in gender), representing the transcendent within the psyche. The significance of the polytheistic phase, which encompassed almost four millennia and expressed the position of highly intellectual cultures as those of Egypt, Greece, and Rome, appears to have been dismissed when the phase faded out of existence, except as represented in myth.[3] And yet, it seems as if a psycho-historical understanding of religion should include a reflection on the psychodynamics that eventuated in a multidimensional configuration of the transcendent, as well as the psychodynamics that replaced it with the current phase of the single Patriarch. Christine Downing (1993), professor of Mythological Studies at Pacifica Institute, recounts the Greek view of the gods as energies that affect everyone and are referred to "as *theos*, that is, as immortal, permanent, ineluctable aspects of the world" (p. 9, italics in the original). She points out that, while disputes among the Greek pantheon were frequent, no god of the Classical era ever denied the existence of another god. And she cautions that to deny even one of the pantheon diminishes the richness of individuals and of the world.

Perhaps the polytheistic tent supported by the concept of the universality of the divine, and enriched by the significant variegated and moderating contribution from its feminine side, has collapsed and with it the recognition of the divine within the "They." The ancient feeling that all believers had of sharing the same spiritual dimension acted as a deterrent against the complete dehumanization of those who differed from the "We." That ancient feeling, which transcended in the spiritual realm the dividing essentialisms of different societies and acted as a Great Mother of sort, has simply disappeared. One has to keep in mind that even if in the predominant moderate reality of our time there is apparent tolerance toward other religions, it is just that:

tolerance; the foundations of tolerance are always subject to the stress from a multiplicity of fault lines, and this precariousness is glaringly evident today.

In addressing this process of dehumanization, Professor Volkan touches upon a point that is a source of apprehension to many: how modernization has enhanced the disconnectedness among humans. This is a theme that applies to so many aspects of our civilization (and we constantly need to remind ourselves that civilization is not culture); a civilization in which the natural propensity toward essentialism has been significantly challenged by complex redefinitions of the core properties and of the concept of boundaries, and that Professor Volkan aptly labels the "who are we now?" civilization.

The fast rate of the present communication system makes it impossible for large groups to remain in isolation, and facilitates global exchanges. At the same time, the constantly growing pressure from the sheer number and speed of communications, achieved at the cost of content and reflection, both of which demand complexity, shrinks the meaning and the reality of human interactions. It offers insufficient time for reflective assessment of the information, and it offers no space for true emotional exchange and interpersonal understanding, because emotions are deconstructed and miniaturized into tiny emoticons that carry almost nothing of the highly complex emotional palette of the sender, and carry everything, by reactive projection, of the emotional palette of the receiver. This approach reflects the widespread reliance on the reductionist scientific method, in this case employed for cognitive as well as affective communication; given the profound limitations of reductionism when applied to the biological domain, the methodology is quite open to misinformation, impulsive evaluations and rash judgments, and cross-boundary conflict. To paraphrase physicist Philip Anderson (1972), the ability to reduce everything to simple fundamental elements does not imply the ability to start from those elements and reconstruct the universe.

Terrorism has also forced upon the world the problem of multiethnicity by creating waves upon waves of displaced and severely traumatized refugees, who add to the anxious confusion of the "who are we now?" question. Because of this substantial foreign influx, numerous fault lines of potential or actual conflict have come into being within large systems that had been accustomed to a dominant essential identity that provided a superficial sense of stability and permanence. Gender, ethnicity, religion, language, culture: the simultaneous interaction of differing expressions of all these properties adds to the anxious confusion and facilitates the calls for retrenchment into essentialist simplifications.

To further complicate the process of assimilation, some individuals among the displaced masses of the refugees may already be conditioned to identify with the aggressor as a sort of vicarious, angry restoration of their deeply wounded narcissism and devalued, crippled sense of selfhood. These persons are particularly susceptible to terroristic recruitment through the seductive message of becoming a God-chosen special hero and "evangelist." Whenever it is discovered that they have become members of some terroristic organization, the hosting society reacts by considering *all* those among the foreigners who look like them as essentially similar, and as potential threats to the national security. The problem of terrorism is real and urgent, and the global, anonymous, and immediate network of communication has magnified its presence, its effects, and the process of recruitment. The solution is still out of sight; but reliance on artificial walls, either concrete or ideological, and the denial of the reality of globalization through the delusion of exclusive essentialism are not workable options.

As a concluding comment on a lighter tone, mythology may offer a more reliable alternative. An ancient tale, mentioned in the *Bibliotheca* of Apollodorus, and captured on an Attic krater[4] tells the story of a "Bin Laden" of those times, a bloodthirsty and cruel prince and "son of Ares" named Cygnus, who was bent on murdering "all foreigners" who happened to pass through his territory in southern Thessaly, who used to steal the offerings intended for the gods, and who caused terror in the region. Heracles—a veritable "Delta Force" of that age—was deployed against him and was eventually able to kill him. However, the death triggered the full activation of "Ares Unbound." The war god marched into the field in all his destructive fury, to avenge the death of his "child." His defeat, the legend says, required the intervention of bolts-throwing Zeus, the supreme representative of the established religious order (the ultimate Ayatollah?), and it required the armed intervention of the goddess Athena, fully vested in her roles as bearer of both wisdom and feminine power.

Perhaps the ancient tale describes crucial aspects that are presently absent in the struggle against terrorism: some reliance on the significant power that the transcendent dimension continues to have on the collective human psyche. The Zeus image suggests the strongest possible condemnation, from the established religious order, of the terrorist desecration of the divine message, to be unequivocally and loudly preached inside the vast tent of the believers, accompanied by the equally strong disavowal of any form of violent radicalism; the Athena image suggests the reliance on the feminine functions, fully liberated from the oppressive burka imposed by the exclusivity of the monotheistic patriarchy, fully reactivated within the psyche to their high original level, and recognized once more as fundamental aspects of the transcendent organization—or "religion" upon which humanity has based its relationship with the "cosmic order of existence" (Geertz, 1993).

NOTES

1. The so-called "nuclear option" adopted by the Republican majority of the US senate in order to accomplish the last Supreme Court appointment is an illuminating example which was discussed by Littman and Flegenheimer, 2017.

2. Freud's largely negative concept of religion was further discussed in "The Future of an Illusion" (1927c), where he concluded that all religious beliefs are illusions although he changed somewhat this negative view in *An Autobiographical Study* (1935), where he stated that while religion's "power lies in the truth which it contains, I showed that that truth was not a material but a historical truth," p. 72.

3. For archetypal psychologists as James Hillman, Joseph Campbell, and Carl Jung, myths about the fabled divinities of old appear to represent the human search for what is true, significant, and meaningful.

4. A krater is a mixing vessel used to mix wine and water before serving. Black-figure pottery painting is one of the styles of painting on ancient Greek (Attic) vases.

Chapter 6

Hateful Feelings in the Transference and Countertransference

Aisha Abbasi

Things happen. In the world we live in, events take place. All kinds of events. We notice these events. So do our patients. Or, at least, we hope they will. If they don't, there's a very serious problem. If they do notice, but do not bring up these events in the therapeutic setting, it's a different kind of problem. Patients need our help with not noticing things, and with not talking about what they notice, for whatever rationalized or irrational, conscious or unconscious reasons.

In this contribution, I will talk about particular periods in my work with three patients, at points when major sociopolitical events occurred in the world. I will share with you how discussing the patients' feelings about these events allowed for a deepening of the clinical work leading us to understand aspects of the patients' history, and their conflicts, in new, unexpected, and meaningful ways. In all the treatments, what patients felt about these external events, was closely related, of course, to their own internal struggles, and to feelings about me in the transference. At the same time, very strong and disturbing feelings came up in me, as I discussed these events with my patients: both because of what the events evoked in me, and because of my reactions to what my patients were saying about these events, and how they were directing certain feelings related to these events, toward me.

MR. BRODSKY

Mr. Brodsky, a Jewish man in his thirties, came to see me in the early years of my analytic career and several years before the events of September 11, 2001. He reported great difficulty with feelings of rage, which resulted in terrible arguments with his wife. His childhood had been marked by a father who had been successful as a businessman early in the patient's childhood, but then sold the business and failed at all other careers, which was witnessed by Mr. Brodsky from the age of ten onward. He had a younger brother and sister and felt that his sister was his parents' favorite. His mother often complained to him about how inadequate his father was as a provider. Mr. Brodsky came to America in his teens, went to college here, joined the human resources department of a company, and married a well-educated Jewish woman whose professional development was hindered by her emotional issues, which seemed to concern Mr. Brodsky—but also made him feel superior to his wife.

He responded to my recommendation for a five-times-a-week analysis on the couch by citing time and financial constraints and began, instead, a four-times-a-week analysis, sitting up. Over the next few months in sessions, Mr. Brodsky talked in a very controlled and controlling way, condescendingly remarking upon my "good work" when I said something that felt useful to him, and wondering how his sitting up was affecting my progression as a new psychoanalytic candidate. He expressed sympathy for the difficult situation I must be in with my supervisor over this matter. In an analytically dutiful way, I asked him his thoughts about all of this but gradually realized that I felt angry, inadequate, controlled, and paralyzed as an analyst with him.

I could now point out to him that he seemed to feel that I had more to lose than he did if he was not fully helped in his analysis. Why was that? Memories emerged of his being held between his mother's knees when he was six years old and a female friend of hers giving him a shot in the buttocks. "I can't use the couch," he said, "because you want me to." He then told me that when he was a teenager, he had tried to physically attack his mother during a fight and had to be held back by two people. In another incident, he had pointed a rifle at his sister, and most recently, before coming to see me, he had kicked his wife in the buttocks (the very part of his body where he had been injected by his mother). His recalling these events in this particular sequence allowed me to share with him my thought that he was afraid that I wanted to humiliate and control him, and was protecting himself by putting me down and controlling the structure of his analysis even if it kept him from using the treatment in the most beneficial manner. These discussions allowed Mr. Brodsky to begin coming to treatment five times a week, although still sitting up. Now his discomfort about feeling attracted to me and experiencing me as his desirable, dark-haired older sister came into the analysis, with worries that he might feel sexually aroused and at my mercy if he were to use the couch.

The greatest shift emotionally, however, was centered on an external event: the Israeli-Palestinian peace accord of 1993, trumpeted in newspapers all over the world by the image of the historic handshake between Yasser Arafat and Yitzhak Rabin. On the day this news broke, Mr. Brodsky brought it up in the session and then could not speak. We then learned that even though he knew I was from Pakistan, he had not allowed himself to "know" that I was a Muslim. All hell now broke forth in the analysis, in a way that ultimately proved to be critically useful. Mr. Brodsky shared with me, with great trepidation, that in school in his early years in America, he had been an active member of a Jewish political group and had organized many anti-Arab and anti-Muslim rallies. His favorite rabbi used to call Muslims "dogs," and he had been raised to believe that all Muslims were anti-Semites. I must see, he said, that we could not possibly work together.

I found myself feeling intrigued by and curious about his responses, but not particularly disturbed; the war between the Muslims and the Jews felt like a remote and distant problem. What, I thought privately, did *I* have to do with that conflict, really? I had grown up in Pakistan, many countries away from the Middle Eastern struggle between the Israeli Jews and the Palestinian Muslims. Since my patient was struggling with these issues, however, and they were very much a part of his personal experience and history, I would certainly try my best to help him with these matters. In retrospect, *it is precisely this lack of internal disturbance on my part, and my attempts to distance myself geographically and emotionally from the conflicts my patient was describing, that should have alerted me that something was amiss with me.*

Instead, I simply said to Mr. Brodsky, quite calmly, that I heard his distrust of me as a Muslim and a possible anti-Semite, his terror of his own hatred and rage, and his fear of mine. But why was it that we could not continue to talk about all of this? He replied thoughtfully that even though we were so different, he felt that I had always been very decent with him; maybe he would be crazy to stay, but perhaps leaving would be foolish. So we continued, Mr. Brodsky and I, external "enemies" engaged in a psychoanalytic process, with the common goal of helping him understand his own suffering.

Sometime after this I changed my car, going from a stripped-down Nissan Sentra to a more luxurious Audi. My Nissan used to make Mr. Brodsky feel that I must be an unsuccessful physician, just as his father had been an unsuccessful businessman. My German Audi was "a lovely color, a great car," he said, "but I would never buy one like that. I call it a Nazi car." I could now interpret more openly Mr. Brodsky's anxieties about what each of us—a male and a female, a Jew and a Muslim—might do to the other were he to deepen his analysis. He now shared with me that in part, his not using the couch made him feel like he had fooled his wife, whom he felt had coerced him into "going into analysis." He felt he was avenging himself by paying to see me but not using the couch: "I'm fooling her. She thinks I am really in analysis, but I'm sort of in and sort of not." I asked, "And how about the way in which you are fooling and hurting yourself?" He said he was only now beginning to see that a little bit. These exchanges between us led Mr. Brodsky to use the couch for the first time, nine months into the analysis. The importance of those nine months, the period of gestation, and his wish for me to "carry" him as the "good-enough mother" (Winnicott, 1971) he had never had, was not lost on either of us.

In the latter part of the third year of Mr. Brodsky's analysis, I needed to stop working on Saturdays, which was one of the days I used to see him. I discussed this with him to see if we could find another time during the week. His reaction was strong and vivid. There was much curiosity about the change and anger about how inconvenient this would be for him. Gradually, associations emerged about the dark-skinned maid who had worked at his parents' house when he was a child. She cleaned the house every weekday, but never came on weekends. I wondered about the derogatory implication of my being "paid help" and wondered whether this was a way for him to deal with his feelings of helplessness and anger about my unavailability over the weekend. He then told me that he had not had a close relationship with this maid; like his mother, she seemed to prefer his sister and his brothers over him. As we talked about this and its link to his current feelings of feeling unimportant with me, he was able to set up a fifth time with me during the week.

A couple of sessions after this, however, he came in on a Monday and told me that something very upsetting had happened over the weekend. He had a cat, which had been his pet since he came to the United States. He kept it in the garage because his wife did not like it. He had never had the cat declawed, and it liked to kill small animals and bring them into the garage. Over the weekend, the cat had attacked a small rabbit and brought it into the garage. The rabbit was still alive, even though the cat had bitten a chunk of flesh out of it, and his wife had pleaded with him to kill the rabbit quickly. Mr. Brodsky spent quite some time in the backyard, deciding how best to do this. Ultimately, he used a shovel to smash the rabbit's head.

As Mr. Brodsky spoke, I became aware that his affect seemed to be one of both fear and excitement. I also noticed that in his "debating" the various merits and demerits of the options available to him for putting the rabbit out of its misery, he had, of course, prolonged its agony. Later that night, at the moment he was about to have intercourse with his wife, she suddenly asked him if he was going to get rid of the cat. He became very angry with her, he told me, and turned away. He added, "I think my analysis must be helping. At another point in the past I would have been tempted to throw her out of the bed, but I didn't. I just turned away from her." I noted the violently angry feelings he sensed toward his wife when he felt she was hitting him "below the belt." I noted also the difficulty he had in putting the rabbit out of its misery, thus prolonging its suffering (an act of sadism, I thought privately). I pointed out the context in which these associations had emerged, a context that was connected to my being unavailable to him over the weekend.

Mr. Brodsky then began to talk about a Muslim woman whom he had dated in college in the United States. He said he had "forgotten" to tell me about this. This was a woman he had known for about a year but never had sex with, because she refused to have a physical relationship with him. He had been strongly attracted to her, but could not get anywhere with her. During the next few days, he talked of his concern about my being alone in the office early in the morning when he came to see me. He said he was worried I would be attacked and raped in the parking lot and he described fantasies of how he would save me. I noted his concern for me, but said that interestingly, he was concerned for me in this fantasy after placing me in a position of danger. It seemed he was struggling enormously with his feelings of needing to protect me *and* his feelings of wanting to hurt me. After a pause, he said he wondered how my husband could allow me to come to the office so early in the morning and that perhaps my husband had divorced me because of my professional goals and ambitions. His thoughts then went to being about ten years old and finding love letters written to his father by a woman with whom his father had been having an affair. He had given these letters to his mother, but, much to his surprise, his mother had not left his father, even though there had been tremendous fights at home between them. His mother had been very angry at him for having told her about this. He felt enraged that she did not appreciate what he had done and had not left his father, about whom she was always complaining.

I noted with Mr. Brodsky that he seemed to want me to have been abandoned by my husband or to have left my husband because of him—to create a separation in my marriage of the kind that had not occurred in his parents' failed marriage, even after he revealed his father's infidelity to his mother. I noted how important it was to him to be important to me and the lengths to which he had to go in his fantasies to achieve this—how unsure he felt of his position with me.

Further associations now began to include thoughts about an affair he had had with a married woman (a white American) after he had first moved to the United States. He described her as being several years older than him and living with her husband and children. She had helped him in many ways during the first few years of being in a country that was foreign to him. One day she came to his apartment after a party, and they made love. Afterward, as she was sleeping with her head on his shoulder, he put his arm around her neck and started bending his forearm, trying to strangle her. After a few moments of doing this he felt "shocked and scared." I said, "Perhaps you recognized how close you came to killing her, and how much that troubled you?" He said, with much feeling, "I loved her and hated her. I loved her for everything she was and what she did for me and I hated her because she was never fully mine. She always had her own life." I asked, "Like your mother?"

and he responded, angrily and with vigor, "Damn you, yes, and like you. And like my sister."

This conversation led to his telling me in great detail, over time, about his beautiful sister, who was accomplished at everything and had a host of admirers following her around. "I felt," Mr. Brodsky said bitterly, "like a little puppy shadowing her." I remembered with a sense of shock that he had told me early in our work that his favorite rabbi used to say that all Muslims were dogs. I brought this up with him, and he said, somewhat self-consciously, but with relief, "So that makes you just like me, I guess, a puppy, a worthless dog who follows people around." I said, "And perhaps also a bitch?" He laughed and responded, "Thank you—actually, yes, I do feel that way sometimes, especially when you have to change my times or cancel a session."

I reflected with him that he had a constant struggle in his mind, between loving and needing a woman and feeling enraged at not having his needs met by her. This created in him not just a sense of anger and rage, but the urge to kill—like his cat, who lived in the garage and killed little animals. My unavailability to him over the weekend seemed to have precipitated the same feeling: that I did not need him as much as he needed me—like his mother, who had chosen to stay with a violent, unfaithful husband while scolding the patient for having caused problems, and the older married woman who stayed with her husband but maintained a sexual relationship with him. The violent cat, I said, with the sharp claws represented an aspect of him, one that worried and frightened him although he felt he could not survive without it. A few weeks after this he started trying to find a home for the cat, and a few months later he gave it away.

We continued to work together, and from time to time his sharp claws would come out again—when he told me he could not increase my fee, for instance, but was giving money to a Jewish charity, or when he wondered whether I would successfully graduate from my analytic training if he were to quit his analysis. We were more able to relate such sadistic attacks on me to his need to deny *his* helplessness and dependence *and* his satisfaction at feeling he had rendered me helpless or was hurting me. Over the course of the analysis, we came to understand much about how Mr. Brodsky's perceptions of me were intricately connected, primarily, to his feelings about his mother and sister, by whom he had felt excluded and hurt and toward whom he felt great rage—rage that was, initially, easier to experience as the righteous, politically determined rage of a Jew toward a Muslim rather than a deep and personally felt rage toward me as a controlling, withholding mother and the sister he loved, wanted, and hated. This, in turn, allowed us to examine his complicated feelings about his father and brother.

HOW I CHANGED AS AN ANALYST AFTER 9/11

To say that the terrible events of 9/11 and their aftermath affected all of us in profound ways does not do justice to the enormity of what happened. On my part, knowing that Muslims had caused such destruction in my adopted country and killed so many innocent people was shocking and, at first, surprising: how could these be "my people?" Was I really one of "those people?" And who, actually, were "my people?" For the first time since my emigration to the United States in 1987, I began to realize that I was both an American and a foreigner to America. In a tentative way, I struggled to understand more of what this event had evoked in me. External events bring forth different responses from each one of us, responses rooted in our personal life histories. The fact that America was connected to a deeply painful, life-altering event in my childhood, and that America was also the country I had adopted as my home in my late twenties—and where I had become a psychoanalyst—took on new and more complex meanings after 9/11. The recognition that my struggle to sort out my alliances and where I belonged was related to childhood struggles—over splits, factions, and divided loyalties in my family of origin—took much longer and is an ongoing effort, as such matters are for most of us.

Then there was, of course, the professional aspect. As an immigrant Muslim analyst of Pakistani origin, my work life took an unexpected turn. My patients started to bring in their intense fear and hatred of Muslims, while turning to me, a Muslim, for help with the terror of their own rage toward the terrorist Muslims and all that they represented. I was put in the curious and difficult position of trying to quickly find my own precarious balance about the events of 9/11 and, at the same time, help my patients find theirs. The devastation caused by the terrorist attacks had breached the necessary boundary between fantasy and reality to a shocking degree, and the "as-if" quality of my patients' transferences toward me was temporarily shattered. They vacillated between imagining, on the one hand, that I was a reliable analyst toward whom they could have destructive wishes, *feeling* that I might retaliate but at the same time knowing, on a deeper level, that I would not, and on the other, feeling that I was an unreliable and dangerous person who came of dangerous stock, and that their hateful feelings toward me might actually cause me to hurt them: after all, look at what my people had just done.

On my part, the sadism and viciousness of the terrorist attacks made old external experiences and my internal responses to them come alive in a way that was new and useful, but also frightening. The "terrorist" parts of me seemed temporarily too real, and in my mind, the boundary between what was fantasy and what was reality felt strained, reminiscent of childhood conflicts.

I listened to my patients, knowing that I was not functioning at my best as an analyst, and tried to sort out my own feelings, while also feeling a need to help my patients, who were distressed and frightened. Together, we navigated the turbulent seas where prejudice, rooted in the innermost recesses of our minds, reigns supreme and threatens to temporarily obscure the search for meaning. I was forced to become more honest with myself, as I struggled to deal with some of my patients' vitriolic attacks against "my" people. How had I managed to deal with Mr. Brodsky relatively calmly, I now wondered, unfazed by his initial attacks on me as a Muslim, only later understanding that they derived from his personal conflicts? I had thought it was because of my great capability to not take things personally. I now realized that it was because I had been what might be best described as the "James Bond martini style" of analyst: shaken, not stirred. I had felt a bit shaken, intrigued by, and curious about Mr. Brodsky but, defensively, had *not* allowed myself to be stirred to the core, to be sufficiently disturbed by him. Yet this is a prerequisite for every truly useful analytic process.

In the wake of 9/11, I also questioned my previously naïve belief that another reason Mr. Brodsky's attacks on me as a Muslim had not bothered me was because I had never met a Jewish person until I came to the United States at the age of 26. What was so alive for him—the danger of our differences—was supposedly not a problem for me. Yet how was this possible? I had grown up in a country where the government and the media clearly sided with the Palestinian Muslims whenever the Israeli-Palestinian issue was discussed. The same was true of discussions I heard at home. I had believed I had no shred of anti-Semitism in me—but now I questioned that belief. I began to take a deeper look at my own prejudice, its origins, and meanings. Which one of us does not have secret prejudices, often connected to our early experiences that we compartmentalize into neatly rationalized categories? And wasn't this what many of my patients were struggling to sort out for themselves in the wake of an external reality that had caused extreme damage and loss and reawakened internal turmoil, albeit somewhat differently in each person?

I will now present process material from the analysis of a male patient I worked with after 9/11.

MR. GUPTA

Mr. Gupta was a 30-year-old Hindu man of Indian origin living in Bangalore, India, who worked as an information technology expert. I had evaluated him a number of years earlier, when he worked in the United States, and at that time, given his childhood history and conflicts about his sexual orientation, I had recommended analysis. He decided instead to meet with me only once a week, citing as a reason that he might be going back to India soon. We met once a week for a year, after which he did indeed go back to India.

I heard from him once after his departure. He asked for a referral to an analyst in India, which I gave him. Ten years later, in February 2009, he called again and told me he had seen a couple of people in the interim period but had not found those treatments helpful, and wanted to begin an analysis. Would I be willing to work with him? And if so, how? I was moved by Mr. Gupta's capacity and need to hold me and my initial recommendation in his mind for ten years, and saddened by his prolonged emotional suffering. I told him that I was now doing some analytic work over the phone and would be happy to speak with him. We could then decide how to proceed.

I was curious as to why Mr. Gupta had contacted me at this time, and learned that his anxieties about feeling sexually attracted only to men—anxieties he had spoken of as a young twenty-year-old—were still alive and well. So were his profound narcissistic vulnerabilities when he felt ignored. In response to my question, "Why now?," Mr. Gupta said that the day before the Mumbai terrorist attacks of November 2008—in which Muslim terrorist attackers invaded India from Pakistan's seawaters and carried out more than ten coordinated shooting and bombing attacks across Mumbai, India's largest city, that had killed 164 and wounded 300—he had been feeling very angry at his boss, who was giving preferential treatment to a colleague of Mr. Gupta's. He was also feeling angry that Arjun, a male colleague he was attracted to, seemed to be vacillating between responding to Mr. Gupta and drawing away from him. Then came the Mumbai terrorist attacks.

He was glad he did not live in Mumbai and wondered how any human being could behave in the way the Muslim terrorists had. I asked how he felt about reconnecting with me—an analyst of Pakistani origin—a few months after the attacks, which had been traced back to Muslims from Pakistan. He said he had been thinking about me a lot over the last few months and feeling more and more that he really wanted help; he should have started an analysis ten years ago, as I had suggested. I thought that immense terror had been unleashed in Mr. Gupta by the combination of his recent mounting anger about being ignored and excluded and the violence and sadism in the terrorist attacks. Did he feel also that I had excluded/abandoned him ten years ago, when he left America to go back to India?

Mr. Gupta's childhood history was still fresh in my mind, with its combination of a professionally successful father who was often out of town and a mother he said he felt loved and helped by, but who would often come out of the shower half-dressed and change her clothes in the parental bedroom, where Mr. Gupta might be watching TV on the bed. Some of his most painful memories had to do with his father ignoring him on family vacations and instead playing cricket with Mr. Gupta's cousins and the sons of family friends, or paying more attention to Mr. Gupta's younger brother, his only sibling. He thought this had to do with his father's view of Mr. Gupta as unathletic and not as funny as his brother.

We then began a telephone analysis five times a week, with the understanding that Mr. Gupta would come to the United States once a year so that we could meet in person. The following session took place a little more than a year into the analysis. The session was to be followed by a ten-day break on my part, which Mr. Gupta had known about for six months. The session below took place on the Friday before my break.

Mr. Gupta began by saying that he had seen a movie, *My Name Is Khan*, the day before. The story was about a couple in New York, a Muslim man and his Hindu wife, whose young son had been beaten to death at a local school shortly after 9/11 because he was Muslim. The wife was enraged and felt that their son had died because her husband was a Muslim. She told him to go and prove to the world that not all Muslims were terrorists. So the hero embarked on a journey, during which he uncovered a Muslim terrorist plot, reported it to the FBI, and, ultimately, met the president.

"He went to such lengths to prove his love for his Hindu wife," I mused, "even exposing other Muslims as terrorists." Mr. Gupta said dismissively that he found the movie preachy and boring. He then went on to talk about a female colleague who wanted to leave the company they both worked for and go to another one, where she thought she might get more perks. He had talked her out of the idea and she was ultimately grateful, because it would have been a self-destructive career move. After a pause, he added that he had played squash that day, which he hadn't done for a long time. His "marker" (the referee's assistant) was happy to see him. "And there's going to be a small party in my honor at work," he added, "to acknowledge how well I have done with this new project."

"It feels good to be wanted and appreciated," I noted. "That makes you feel very glad." He laughed and said that it sure did. I wondered about his laughter at this moment. He said, "You said something I was feeling, but could not say. I felt a little embarrassed that you picked up on it—this feeling of wanting to be wanted. How good it feels to be wanted." A long silence followed. He seemed to be thinking, struggling to say something. "I've been reading about this list of fourteen countries," he finally said, "Cuba and thirteen Muslim countries, whose passengers must be scanned by these new body scanners before they can enter the U.S. I wondered if you are an American citizen. But even if you are, you would have to be scanned, especially if you were traveling back to the U.S. from Pakistan. You must go back to visit your family from time to time."

"Perhaps that's where I'll be when I am not here next week?" I asked. "I did think that," he acknowledged. "I read that some Muslim women in England refused to go through the body scan." Silence. "But then, if they want to get on a flight, they have to allow themselves to be searched. Then the passenger is at the mercy of the authorities. They can even do body-cavity searches, you know." I heard the indirect, ominous threat he was directing against me, his wish for me to be viciously intruded upon and humiliated, disguised as a "helpful" warning from him that I should be prepared for my body cavities to be searched upon my return from the trip he imagined I was embarking on—the trip that was causing a separation between us. I listened.

"India is not on this list," Mr. Gupta continued. "And I've been having many thoughts about what you think about the Indian/Pakistani issue? The enmity. What if your thoughts are different from mine? What would happen to my analysis then? Sometimes, I feel you're a very hotheaded person. Certain things seem to get you all stirred up. I've noticed that sometimes when I talk about someone putting me down and I haven't asserted myself, you start talking to me in a way that makes me think you could get very agitated or angry, and I wonder what you'd be like, if you were very angry." There was a brief pause.

"I'm thinking," he said, "about the Mumbai terrorist attacks last year." I said he had called me, looking for help again, very soon after those attacks. He responded, "Yes, exactly. And I know that the information India finally uncovered was that the terrorists belonged to Lashkar-e-Tayyaba, originally located in Pakistan—that the entire plot was planned in Pakistan. But what if we disagree about where the terrorists came from? What if I insist that they were Muslims trained in Pakistan, and you don't want to see it that way? It's one thing when you get all animated trying to help me assert myself, but what if you get really angry as we speak about these major issues we might think very differently about? I don't want to piss you off. I mean, most of the time, I think this is really cool that I am an Indian Hindu and I have an analyst who is a Muslim and originally from Pakistan, and here we are, working together. That's pretty cool."

"Sometimes it feels pretty cool to you, and at other times, you feel it could be very, very dangerous," I said. Silence. Then Mr. Gupta said, "I've been invited to attend a fundraiser for an Indian NGO [non-governmental organization]. The President of the NGO is a guy named Bashir Iqbal [a Muslim name]. He hasn't invited me personally. I'm not sure I want to go. I would be someone brought in from the outside, my presence there arranged by our marketing department. But I am not a part of that organization." A pause. "I snubbed Arjun [the man at work whom Mr. Gupta was attracted to, but from whom he was not getting a consistent positive response] today, didn't invite him to join me and a few other colleagues when we were headed out for lunch. He's done that to me at times."

"So much here about inclusion and exclusion," I reflected. "Who's part of the 'in crowd,' who's invited, who's not, and who gets to be with whom. You feel a sense of great hurt when you feel left out or rejected and you automatically take certain steps to ensure that the tables are turned—that you're the one in control and the other person feels snubbed." "Oh, I really don't have a serious problem with these things," Mr. Gupta retorted. "I just dealt with Arjun and made sure that he felt uncertain and unwelcome." "Just as *you* felt around *him*," I interjected quietly. "And yet you don't *really* have a problem with this *at all*."

There was a long silence. I wondered if what I had confronted him with made him feel too exposed. When he spoke, he sounded angry and defensive. "I'm just preventing further pain," he said. "He's the one who invited me to dinner last year when we were in England and then would send me text messages talking about the great times we'd had there. But then he became distant and I feel he's not even sincere with me, nor is he really concerned about me." He was quiet. "Okay, I guess you're right. I just repeated what you had actually said. But what the hell else am I supposed to do when I feel left out?" I remained quiet. "I wish we could continue talking next week. This is hard to deal with, all these bad feelings I have when I feel ignored or pushed aside."

"As when I go away and am not here for you," I said. Silence. Then Mr. Gupta said, "I am wondering how it is for you now in America? Are you being discriminated against? Do people think you might be crazy, like a terrorist? I found myself thinking the other day, do people even call you to see you for treatment? Or do they feel they don't want to come to you for analysis because you're a Muslim from Pakistan?" I now felt the full onslaught of Mr. Gupta's sadistic retaliatory attack—his attempt to regain his narcissistic equilibrium in the storm of feeling belittled by being left. He had tapped into the most primitive anxieties I had felt after 9/11, anxieties connected to my personal history and reawakened by the external events of 9/11 and its aftermath.

I paused, swallowed hard, and asked, "And what might happen to me then?" He responded in a matter-of-fact way, as though he were reading some headlines from the newspaper. "Oh, I think you'd be completely wiped out professionally then. Maybe you wouldn't get any patients—and then I suppose you wouldn't have any money, either." "And that would serve me right, wouldn't it?" I asked, finding now more stable analytic ground. "For leaving you. It's satisfying for you when you imagine I might be subjected to having my bodily orifices intruded upon and violated, or that I might be wiped out professionally—and you speak about it so calmly." "I don't feel very calm," he said. "I feel very agitated. Actually, I was thinking just now that maybe that's why you agreed to work with me in analysis—because you wanted to make money, and no one else wanted you as their analyst."

I heard his comment, designed to be hurtful and insulting, but covering over his hurt that I might have agreed to see him for ulterior motives, and his deep disbelief that he could be wanted, or loved, for himself. I said, "Yes, because if that were so, then you'd be my *only* patient, wouldn't you?" I asked. "And very, very special to me. I would really want you. Not like the way you felt with your parents." After a long silence, Mr. Gupta spoke. "All my life," he said, "these difficult, sad feelings with so many people, so many real disappointments and rejections. I do wonder sometimes if I imagine now that people are mistreating me even when they're not, people like you who are actually trying to help me."

It was also only later that I could understand, with Mr. Gupta, that his sadistic fantasy of my bodily orifices being viciously searched and attacked had to do not only with his rage at feeling excluded from my life and my body, but also his wish to find a way into me and within me, with a loving, sexual longing.

AGNES

I no longer believe, in fact have not for several years now, that we should talk to patients only about what they want to talk about with us. I consider this a distortion of the idea of free association. I am just *as* interested in, and sometimes *more* interested in, what a patient is *not* saying, or does *not* want to talk about, because in many instances, the most significant communications are not in what patients tell us, but in what they don't.

On the night of Tuesday, November 8, as I watched on TV the voting results coming in from various states, it became increasingly clear that much to my surprise, and that of many other Americans, our country was turning "red." I went to bed around midnight, certain that next morning, America would no longer be the country I had migrated to, almost thirty years ago. And it was not. How much this country would change, though, I could not have anticipated, and had to rapidly learn, and try to deal with, over the next few months, each of which now often feels like a year.

Most of the patients in my practice reported voting Democrat. Two did not: one a man, and the other a woman. For this presentation, I have chosen to present material from my female patient, since the other patients I have talked about today, are men. And also because the very difficult and tumultuous feelings that came up in the treatment of this young woman, on both sides of the therapeutic dyad, are very illustrative of the kind of issues that are the topic of this chapter.

Agnes is a beautiful woman, in her early forties, and of Polish descent. Her grandparents migrated to this country. She is married to a man, also of eastern European descent, who, through his business skills, became very wealthy, very quickly, something the couple savor and enjoy. They have two children. Agnes is a homemaker, who prides herself on her culinary and homemaking skills, and is socially adept at helping her husband expand his business. Her parents divorced when she was about seven (the marriage having been very stormy), partially as a result of her father's severe mood problems and alcoholism. She was the older of three children at that time, the other two being boys. She described her mother as being "loving in her own way" but highly judgmental and self-righteous. Her mother remarried shortly after the divorce, and she and her new husband had four more children, all boys, within a short span of time.

Agnes first came to see me, in her late thirties, because of feelings of depression and anxiety. I could hear her pain about the father who had abandoned the family, her need to hold tight to her mother as the parent who remained available (while often feeling criticized and intruded upon by the mother) and her difficult role as the always good and responsible older sister in what eventually became a family of seven. She got married at the age of 34, had children soon thereafter, and was worried about being a good mother for them. Although she loved her husband, her envy of him, and his business and money-making skills, came through. I recommended an analytic treatment, which she expressed interest in, but cited many scheduling difficulties, given her responsibilities for her children, and socially, helping her husband with his clients. I felt she had extreme anxiety about a deeper treatment, and we started at once a week, which she said she could manage. Over the following years, whenever the material allowed, we tried to better understand these anxieties. She would declare she really wanted to come more often: I was so helpful to her, she wanted to understand herself more, etc., etc. Then she would ask to come in twice a week, and even three times a week, but this would have to be reduced back to once a week, because of "scheduling conflicts."

Over time, I felt that she would most likely continue and end her treatment at a once-a-week frequency. Her symptoms improved considerably, she felt happier about how she was mothering her kids, and felt her marriage was stable until her husband started expressing thoughts of wanting to leave her. This led to great pain and anger on her part, and again, during this time, she asked to come in three times a week. The couple also went into marital therapy, and started discussing what had led to this alienation in the marriage. Her husband shared with her that particularly during her pregnancies, but also otherwise, he often found her to be emotionally detached and removed from him, as though she didn't have, and didn't want to have, a sense of what he was feeling, and struggling with. She talked about how she often hid her feelings from him, because he seemed to find her feelings too intense, and her too needy. Many painful, but honest and useful conversations took place between them, and they decided to stay together. As the marriage re-stabilized, she again decreased her sessions to once a week.

By Friday after the November 2016 elections, I had spent two and a half days listening to my patients' reactions to the results of the election and to having Donald Trump as their president. Many reactions were similar for most patients (shock, incredulity, fear, amazement, disbelief, anger, etc.), but each led to associations that ultimately had to do with the very personal history of each patient. One thing was common to all: nobody came in after the elections and said nothing about the elections. Except Agnes.

Agnes started her once-a-week Friday session that week by telling me that her mother had been visiting them over the last few days. Her mother repeatedly asked how things were going in her marriage. Agnes was annoyed by this, but did not say anything about her annoyance to her mother, lest she upset her mother. Finally, over dinner yesterday, when her mother broached the subject again, Ryan, Agnes' husband, told his mother-in-law very firmly that they would prefer to keep discussions about their marriage private, thanks for her concern, but she did not need to worry about things on their behalf, since she could see that both he and Agnes were obviously working at their relationship. Agnes said she realized she had really wanted Ryan to stand up to her mother, since she felt unable to do so. I wondered about this. This was something we had been working at in her treatment, for a long time. She said she was still often afraid her disagreement would disrupt her mother's good mood, and cause her to love her, Agnes, less.

I listened. After a while, she started talking about an older woman at an institution where Agnes volunteers. The woman was doing something wrong, but again, Agnes found it hard to say something to her, even though her position allowed her to do so. I asked again, about her trepidation. She said, again, that she was worried it would offend the woman. Then a silence. I noted the silence. She said she wasn't clear about what she was feeling. Another silence. We were almost twenty-five minutes into the session. I now brought up with her that as she was talking about women she was afraid she would offend, I was realizing that she had not yet said a word about something very significant that had happened in our country this week. She became visibly tense, her posture stiffened, and she said "I am not talking about the elections. I didn't bring that up. Why are you bringing it up?"

I said, "It is exactly because *you* are not talking about it, that *I* am. One of us needs to talk about it, because I think that what you *have* been talking about, and what you have *not* been talking about, both, may be linked to my question." I added that I thought at times like these, the idea that the therapist should only follow the patient's spoken lead in terms of what was discussed, could create a caricature of therapy. And that I find often, that what is *not* talked about, is as much a communication as what *is* talked about. She relaxed a bit, then said, "I voted for Trump. I can't imagine you did. I am almost sure you wouldn't, given what I know about you. And his views about Muslims, and immigrants. I actually considered not voting for him, even though, as a Catholic, I always vote Republican [I had been aware of this], but then I thought that if my mother found out, she'd be really angry. And even Ryan . . . because he likes the idea that Trump will lower taxes for businesses and for the wealthy."

I said "It feels like such a bind for you. To have your own opinion and to express it, is to risk losing the love and approval of people you care about. Perhaps including me?" She responded, "Yes. Now I am thinking: are *you* going to feel mad at me because I voted for Trump? And I am suspicious about why you are asking me these questions. Would you, for instance, ask me this if you thought I had voted for Hillary?" I noted, "You suspect my motives. It's hard to imagine I might ask all my patients their thoughts about why they vote the way they do, and what each candidate means to them. Or that it might be useful, in therapy, for us to understand your leaning in one direction versus another." After a brief silence, she said "Well, I know Trump has problems; but he also has a lot of charisma." I responded, "I see. Tell me, what seems especially charismatic to you?" Agnes said, very brightly, "He always tells it like it is! And I really like that about him." Silence. "Because, you know, I am just like that: I always speak my mind, even if people don't like it. So for me, that was my big draw to him, that we are both the same in that way." She repeated, "We say it like it is!"

I sat back in my chair, my mind spinning. I felt I could not believe what Agnes had just said, nor could I let myself fully believe the extent of the splits within her mind. "Agnes," I said, leaning forward a bit, "Which ***you*** are you talking about?" "What do you mean?" she asked, affronted. "Exactly what I said, "I responded." All through this session, you've been talking about how frightening it feels for you to speak up about what you're thinking and feeling, with your mother, your husband, and with me. Now you are saying, as though we hadn't just talked about all of that, that you always speak your mind, and so does Trump. So I am totally confused by this contradiction, which does not seem to confuse you *at all*. That is why I am asking: which you is it, who always speaks her mind?"

A heavy silence enveloped the room. I found myself feeling, suddenly, a sense of horror, at what I realized had been an ongoing difficulty on *my* part, about fully appreciating the brittleness of my patient; how she compartmentalized, in fact, split off , different feeling states, and pieces of reality, one from the other, and thus was able to maintain a veneer of outward intactness.

I began to appreciate fully, perhaps for the first time in our five years of working together mostly once a week, how terrifying it must be for her to consider being in an intensive treatment, where such divisions in her mind, created for protective reasons, of course, would ultimately have to be recognized, confronted, understood, and dealt with. Agnes started crying softly. "I know" she said, "I know it is so. But I don't know any different. I cannot imagine anyone listening to whatever I have to say, and tolerating it, tolerating me." I said this was really sad, that she could not trust anyone fully, and that even here, in the treatment, she couldn't imagine she might have, with me, a place, where she could be heard, and attended to, and cared about, no matter what her opinions were. She cried again, and said "I want to believe it, I really do, but that has never been my experience," and went on to tell me about a Middle Eastern woman, a friend of hers, who was here on a work permit. This woman, Laila, got very angry at Agnes recently, when she asked Agnes, a few weeks ago, who she would vote for. When Agnes told her, Laila said "I can't believe you would do that: vote for somebody who will most likely cause me and others like me to lose their work permits. How can you call yourself my friend?" And after that, Laila refused to answer her phone calls. I noted she was obviously afraid the same would happen here between us. She said that was usually how it went with her mother as well.

In the next session, a week later, Agnes and I talked further about what we had discussed the last time, and I shared with her my sense that over the last few years, not only she, but I too, had backed off from getting more clearly into the stuff we were now getting into. I had thought privately that it was very rare for me to have a patient who came only once a week, and yet with her, that is what had happened. In some way, a part of me had colluded with a part of my patient, so that despite my intermittent efforts at engaging her in an analysis, I had not been able to do so in the authentic way I do with many other patients. It was as though I had made the right noises from time to time, but had felt secretly relieved that she did not want to be in an analysis. I was now beginning to see and understand my unconscious backing away from deeper involvement with her. And as I began to understand it, propelled by the events of the week of the 2016 elections, I could bring it up with my patient more clearly.

I said to her that this was a painful and difficult way to live, the way she was. It took great emotional energy to maintain such divisions in one's mind, and there was, consequently, less emotional availability for immersion in creativity, joy, love, and intimacy. She felt she was already aware of living in a very constrained way "as though I'm walking on a tightrope." After some more reflection, Agnes decided that she would start a four-times-a-week analysis, and I added two evening hours and a weekend hour to accommodate her until there was a regular opening in my schedule. We had already been on this schedule for a few weeks when the new president had his inauguration on January 20, 2017. Then came President Trump's first travel ban on Friday, January 27, 2017.

Over the weekend that followed, all kinds of chaos ensued for Muslims trying to enter America. Because of the lack of understanding and preparation of the Immigration agents, many Muslims were wrongfully refused entry into the United States that weekend, including those who were Permanent Residents (green card holders), or had valid work visas. I received news of, and calls from, many families affected by this chaos, including many young doctors/residents in training who had gone back to their home countries for a visit and now could not return to their jobs in the United States. I also heard on NPR about a woman from Yemen, who had dual citizenship, had lived in this country a long time, could not speak English very well, and had her American passport confiscated by Immigration agents.

At a local meeting following that weekend, ACLU attorneys explained that for naturalized citizens, their American passports actually belonged to the State Department, and could be taken away at any time. Hardly a comforting thought for me, and one that led me to wonder, very seriously: could my family and I now really think of this country as our home? I had thought I could, but I was now feeling extremely unsure of that, vulnerable, and insecure, as were many other Muslims. Questions were also being raised in the media about why Pakistan was not included in this ban. The thought that one might be imposed, and the possibility that traveling back and forth to my motherland might become a huge and risky challenge, if not impossible, for a long period of time, was also deeply disturbing for me.

Good friends from various communities called to check on me and my family. Most of my patients, whatever their ambivalent feelings about me, and whatever their pleasure at the idea of my possible suffering, nonetheless acknowledged awareness of the ban, and of its possible consequences for me, my family, and my Muslim friends. They were worried for me, and also concerned about themselves and their analyses with me. When Agnes came in on the Tuesday following the imposition of that travel ban, however, she looked calm, serene, and happy. She had just had a wonderful and fun lunch, she said, with a few friends. Over the weekend, she and Ryan swam in their indoor pool, hung out with the kids, then went out for a dinner date, after which they made love. From the couch, her voice became dreamy, content with the pleasure of this carefree weekend. It had been such a perfect weekend, she said. She couldn't imagine a better one.

Sitting behind her, I felt shocked by the grotesque contrast between the publicly known suffering of the thousands of travelers stranded in chaos and misery, families separated, people whose jobs were lost/taken away, all in one weekend; people who belonged to the same ethnic/religious group that

I, her analyst, did and Agnes' calm and satisfied description of *her* weekend. I was also aware of my own profound anxieties about my life now as a naturalized American citizen, my worries about my husband, a Muslim man, as he went about his business every day, and the vulnerability of our brown-skinned children, whom Agnes had seen outside my home at times. I experienced her in that moment as callous and uncaring, smug, and self-satisfied with her safe and lovely life. Then I thought, with some hope: was she perhaps unaware of what had happened around the country and in the world, over this past weekend? Had she completely missed out on the news? So, at some point during the session, I asked her. She said, with surprise "No, why would you think that? Of course I know about that. But I just wanted to tell you what a good weekend I had with Ryan and the family. Should I not talk about that?" I said I thought that in asking me that, she might be wanting to give me enough rope to hang myself with. After all, I had always asked her to say what was on her mind, and so she was. How could I now want her to talk about what might be on *my* mind? That was not how analysis worked, surely, and wasn't I her analyst after all?

At the same time, I noted, there was a tremendous irony in the fact that here she was, with her Muslim analyst, whom she professed had helped her a lot, whom she even professed to love; and that something had happened over the weekend that she could imagine might have affected me deeply, or by extension, my friends and family, but she did not seem at all interested in acknowledging that. It was very puzzling, I said. She had often said she loved me and felt grateful to me. Where was her sense of empathy for me now, I wondered, in terms of a basic awareness of, and acknowledgment of, the situation of uncertainty and helplessness that I, and many other Muslims here, were currently in?

She replied angrily that she didn't care, she didn't want to *have* to care about me. She'd always had to do that with her mother, and she was sick of it. I said "It feels to you that I am asking you for your sympathy and help because I need it. Just like your mother. It's difficult for you to grasp that I consider the emergence of this in the analysis to be very useful . . . that what I am primarily trying to understand is your complete lack of concern or curiosity about me, a person you claim you feel deeply helped by. I am trying to understand this part of you, how this has developed, and what can we learn from this, about your difficulties in other intimate relationships? But it seems that, for now, I may have to be all alone with my curiosity about this curious state of affairs."

Agnes looked thoughtfully and quietly ahead of her. Then she said, tearfully, "This is what Ryan was talking about in our marital therapy: that I become so removed from him at times, focused only on my needs and pleasures. It's true. It really is." "And yet," I said, "you are not an uncaring person; but the caring part of you seems to get totally lost from time to time, with me, and with your husband. There must be reasons for that, for the way you ignore others' needs and pain."

She responded vehemently and angrily, "Yes, yes there is! One is my mother, always demanding stuff—emotional stuff—that she needs from me. And then I think about my brothers, all of them. So many of them. Especially once my parents had the four younger ones, I was just forgotten about, I could wait, I was supposed to make do. If I had a sport event, or a performance, and so did they, well guess what, where do you think my parents went? To my brothers' events, of course! Because they were younger, and I was older, I was supposed to be reasonable." Her voice rose, agitatedly, "But *I was always getting trumped by them*, over and over again."

"So deeply painful, and at times, humiliating, I am sure, for you. What a lot you have suffered through. So maybe it feels good to not be on the receiving end of that cruel neglect, that sense of uncertainty about your place in the world. How much better today, to be the one who gets to be all happy and serene while I and thousands of others like me, are getting 'trumped' by Trump. So important that of all the words you could have chosen today to describe being ignored, to talk about who loses, and who wins, you use this particular word, which takes us right to the heart of what happened in this country over the weekend, and because of whom. How do *I* like it now? To be the outsider, to be trumped by you, and others like you, I the ignored and helpless minority, while you are in control and included in the majority. I think it feels like a useful way, to you, of gaining some control over your feelings about those painful, out of control, humiliating experiences while you were growing up."

DISCUSSION

There is both a fear of and fascination with differences and strangeness; this is universal, yet individually determined for each of us. These may include the patient's perception of differences in gender, external appearances, ways of thinking, skin color, racial background, cultural background, and religion. To understand the individual meanings these differences have for the patient, starting from the most superficial and accessible and going toward the deepest underpinnings, is one of the tasks of an analysis. Can such a task be accomplished in the presence of gross and obvious differences between the patient and analyst that preclude a shared understanding of a common racial/cultural/religious/ethnic background? Perspectives on this issue have varied over time.

Oberndorf (1954) did not think it was possible: "Transference in its most positive form," he wrote, "is most likely to be easily established and examined (analyzed) between patient and hospital and patient and physician if their psychological biases do not differ too widely" (p. 757). The belief seemed to be that people coming from different racial backgrounds would be too distant "psychologically" to be able to establish a transference in the analysis that could facilitate an understanding of the patient's conflicts:

> The fear of the stranger, originating in a young child's feeling of security in the accustomed, and need for protection in the face of the unfamiliar person or place, are [*sic*] almost instinctive . . . the integration of the mentally disturbed individual can best be achieved if he is treated by one of those who understands his motivations rather than by one considered expert in a particular illness. (pp. 757–758)

The thinking here seemed to have been that a patient's motivations could only be understood by someone from a similar cultural background. Between Oberndorf's 1954 paper and the late 1990s, psychoanalytic literature included only a small group of papers on the impact of cultural, ethnic, racial, or religious differences between analyst and patient. Yet this has always been an important issue in the United States, since many early analysts were immigrants. There may be many reasons for this paucity of literature, a discussion of which is not within the scope of this chapter. Its scarcity, however, does not detract from our recognition of its importance. Such differences may have influenced analyses conducted by early immigrant analysts and, later on, as analysts began to write about the experiences of white analysts with black patients, and vice versa. Eventually, other analyst/analysand ethnic combinations attracted attention in the literature as well. This has become even more important today, as the candidate population at psychoanalytic institutes diversifies and more patients from diversified ethnic backgrounds enter psychoanalytic treatment.

In the almost sixty years since Oberndorf presented his paper, the way we think about cross-cultural treatment has evolved. Several analysts have attempted, in detailed, scholarly, and moving papers, to describe their experiences of working in a cross-cultural analytic dyad (Akhtar, 1995, 2006; Goldberg, Myers, and Zeifman, 1974; Holmes, 1992; Leary, 1995, 1997a, 1997b, 2000, 2007). For instance, Schachter and Butts (1968) presented a point of view that was quite different from Oberndorf's:

> Racial differences between analyst and patient involve issues of unconscious meaning at various levels, analogous to differences in sex between analyst and patient. They must be recognized and utilized, but only rarely do they create an either unanalyzable hurdle or a serious obstacle to treatment. (p. 802)

Specific issues requiring close attention come up in analyses that take place across ethnic boundaries. In a 1984 paper, Eva Basch-Kahre, a Swedish analyst, described her work with a black African man living in Sweden. In such contexts, she believes that the analyst's lack of knowledge with regard to the specifics of development, childrearing, values, and conventions of the analysand's background make the "analyst blind to those minimal features which usually alert him that the analysand is approaching conflict territory. I believe that these difficulties cause analysis to proceed at a slower pace, but do not thwart it" (p. 61). I agree, and would extend this to include the fact that particular differences between analyst and patient may cause a kind of "cloudiness" on the analytic horizon, which makes it difficult for the analyst to see things that would be more obvious in other analyses; in such cases, obvious differences between the analytic dyad and the meanings those differences have for patient and analyst may not carry the same weight.

In talking about interracial analysis, Fischer (1971) wrote:

> I am suggesting that the black-white difference between the analyst and analysand is a contributing and visible structure upon which the more basic and dynamic infantile wishes are projected. To ignore or overestimate either the manifest structure or the latent projection leads to an incomplete comprehension and working through. (p. 736)

With my patients as well, the obvious difference between us presented a visible structure onto which they could project their feelings of exclusion and devaluation—feelings they had suffered from in their own lives. This projection was made initially through the lens of the obvious differences between us. In this regard, Ticho (1971) wrote:

> There is no doubt that cultural differences play an important role in psychoanalytic treatment. However, it is the patient who makes his own choice among the many available stereotypes and endows the analyst with certain positive and negative attributes according to his pathology, individual needs and, concomitantly, with the development of the transference neurosi." (p. 315)

Given the increasing numbers of analysts from different ethnic backgrounds, it is essential that close attention be paid to the issue of the developing analyst's comfort or discomfort in dealing with factors related to differences of ethnicity, culture, and religion. The ability to handle this material with patients increases as the analyst better understands his or her own prejudices and conflicts about ethnicity, religion, and culture; this constitutes important work in one's own personal/training analysis. Bernard (1953) made important recommendations with regard to the contribution of the training analysis and supervision in terms of cross-cultural issues. She wrote:

> We know that the personal and training analysis provides the major safeguard against prejudice, but often the unconscious foundations of prejudice have not been worked with adequately. This may be due in part to controversies that exist as to the analytic handling of such material and its relevance to the etiology of neurosis. . . . If, therefore, an analyst has insufficiently analyzed his own unconscious material pertaining to his own group membership and that of others, he and his patient may be insufficiently protected from the interference of a variety of positive and negative countertransference reactions stimulated by the ethnic, religious and racial elements that are present in the analytic situation, the patient's personality, and in the specific content of the patient's material. The supervisory process in analytic training provides a potentially valuable second line of defense for supplementing the personal analysis in regard to these countertransference risks, provided the supervising analyst is himself sufficiently informed and psychologically qualified in these areas. (pp. 258–259).

In a lovely and useful paper, "Anti-semitism in the clinical setting: transference and countertransference dimensions," Knafo (1999) describes a Jewish man whose parents were concentration-camp survivors and whose most exciting sexual fantasies had to do with "naked women about to die in Nazi gas chambers, at which point he achieved orgasm" (p. 38). Knafo, who was then a doctoral candidate, "inwardly recoiled in horror and fear" (p. 38) and could not work with the patient when she realized that in telling her these fantasies, he was excited by including *her* in the fantasy during the session. In later years, Knafo was able to see that "anti-Semitism can be a valuable means of engaging the analysis of transference reactions" (p. 57), and recognized that negative transference reactions, "when embedded in anti-Semitic terminology, tend to be avoided by therapists and analysts" (p. 58). She writes, "I believe this results from the therapist's inability to move beyond the perception of a patient's anti-Semitism as solely a social phenomenon to being able to treat it as he or she would any other clinical manifestation" (p. 58), and adds, "The great challenge for psychoanalysts, I believe, lies in the capacity to bridge social and psychic reality in order to discover what is most therapeutically useful for the patient" (p. 60). I believe that the same holds true for anti-Muslim sentiments expressed in the analytic setting.

CONCLUDING REMARKS

In India and Pakistan, henna (an herbal paste) is mixed with water and applied to the hands of women for certain festive occasions, including weddings. The henna, which is green in the powder and paste form, is left on the skin for several hours and is then removed; the dye seeps into the skin and colors it. The color it becomes on the skin of one woman can be quite different from the color on another: on certain skin tones, the henna is pale orange, and on others, it shows up as bright, flame-colored orange. It is said that on certain hands, the henna "takes" better than on others. It is postulated that the color it becomes depends on some quality intrinsic to the skin.

So it is, I believe, in psychoanalysis: all patients—and all analysts—are "different" from each other, but in each analysis, the use to which the patient and the analyst put these differences is determined by the patient's needs and conflicts. In some analyses, the differences may not emerge in bright colors; in others, they might present in almost dizzying hues because, for the patient, they serve a critical defensive function. I have presented in this contribution vignettes from three analyses in which the ethnic difference between my patients and myself became a vehicle through which their feelings of hurt, rage, and sadism came into the analysis. *This was how the ethnic differences between us were put to use.* I also elaborated on how I could more effectively feel and process my patients' sadistic attacks on me post-9/11, due to my internally increased awareness of *my own* conflicts regarding rage and sadism during that time.

Chapter 7

From Rage to Obliteration

Prejudice in the Analytic Dyad

Suzanne Benser

Chapter 6 of this book, "Hateful Feelings in the Transference and Countertransference," takes the reader deeply into the analytic processes of three patients who enact hateful attacks that range from openly dehumanizing characterizations of Dr. Aisha Abbasi's gender, ethnicity, and religion to silent obliteration of her humanity. Through the clinical material, Dr. Abbasi demonstrates her approach to working with psychosocial concerns in the therapeutic relationship, while illustrating some of the processes that engender and perpetuate prejudice.

The chapter spans Dr. Abbasi's thirty-year career, giving the reader an opportunity to see her analytic identity evolve in tandem with the powerful changes that have occurred in Western culture and psychoanalysis over the past several decades. Dr. Abbasi's description of her analytic self before 9/11 as "cool, like James Bond" channeled neutrality, a key tenant of classical psychoanalytic technique. She evocatively described how the traumatic reality of 9/11 shook her personal and professional core assumptions. Through processing repeated experiences of overt prejudice in our country since 9/11, Dr. Abbasi described how she became aware of her own buried prejudice: "Which one of us does not have secret prejudices, often connected to our early experiences, that we compartmentalize into neatly rationalized categories?" Dr. Abbasi's description of the elusive nature of prejudice foreshadowed the last clinical vignette in which she discovered she had been colluding in an ongoing racist enactment that only came fully into awareness once she confronted the omission in the patient's material of two significant sociopolitical events.

All major psychoanalytic theoretical orientations acknowledge the mutual, reciprocal effects of internal and external realities, and also agree that a basic aim of psychoanalysis is to understand the interplay between the two realities.

However, there is disagreement among the major orientations regarding optimal approaches for distinguishing and elucidating the interplay of internal and external realities (Christopoulos, 2014). Dr. Abbasi's clinical approach of introducing sociopolitical material, along with careful attention to the meaning of omitted material in herself and her patients, presents an approach that she has found clinically valuable, and places her psychoanalytic work in a larger sociopolitical context.

Jeffrey Prager (2015) summarized Vamik Volkan's perspective on working clinically with prejudice:

> Personal identity expresses the human capacity to situate oneself along the continuum of history, and is powerfully defined, or even eclipsed, by the local political and cultural constructs. Individual identity formation becomes shaped and profoundly compromised by the centrality of an exogenous, bigger-than-self large-group identity. The powerful irrational role that "large-group identity" holds over individuals is the source of deeply held hatreds for other groups. However, identification with larger identities, however all encompassing, never can totally usurp the uniqueness or idiom of an individual. (p. 504)

Dr. Abbasi illustrated her ability to work with the interplay of individual identity and large group identity in the first vignette with Mr. Brodsky:

> this led to his telling me in great detail, over time, about his beautiful sister, who was accomplished at everything and had a host of admirers following her around. "I felt," Mr. Brodsky said bitterly, "like a little puppy shadowing her." I remembered with a sense of shock that he had told me early in our work that his favorite rabbi used to say that all Muslims were dogs. I brought this up with him, and he said, somewhat self-consciously, but with relief, "So that makes you just like me, I guess, a puppy, a worthless dog who follows people around." I said, "And perhaps also a bitch?" He laughed and responded, "Thank you—actually, yes, I do feel that way sometimes, especially when you have to change my times or cancel a session."

The vignette captured the interplay of his feelings of self-denigration in relation to his admired sister, and a large group identification that openly denigrates Muslims and covertly denigrates women. A later interaction about Mr. Brodsky's murderous feelings toward an older female lover revealed further details of his destructiveness toward women and his inability to separate from developmental objects:

> Perhaps you recognized how close you came to killing her, and how much that troubled you? He said, with much feeling, "I loved her and hated her. I loved her for everything she was and what she did for me and I hated her because she was

never fully mine. She always had her own life." I asked, "Like your mother?" and he responded, angrily and with vigor, "Damn you, yes, and like you. And like my sister."

Donald Winnicott (1969, 1971) addressed developmental difficulties with separation in his writings on the "use" of an object. He described the developmental transition from perceiving objects as under one's control (object relating) to recognizing objects external to the self (object usage) as a maturational capacity that is not inborn. Winnicott (1971) viewed this aspect of development as dependent on a facilitating environment, and described the process of giving up on attempting to control the subjectively perceived object as "the most difficult thing, perhaps, in human development; or the most irksome of all the early failures that come for mending" (p. 120).

An example of a failure in Mr. Brodsky's facilitating environment that would have contributed to difficulties in his development was described in the following passage:

> His thoughts then went to being about ten years old and finding love letters written to his father by a woman with whom his father had been having an affair. He had given these letters to his mother, but, much to his surprise, his mother had not left his father, even though there had been tremendous fights at home between them. His mother had been very angry at him for having told her about this. He felt enraged that she did not appreciate what he had done and had not left his father, about whom she was always complaining.

The falseness of his mother's response to the father's affair likely contributed to an ongoing "failure of faith" in the realness of self and others as described in Emmanuel Ghent's (1990) furthering of Winnicott's developmental theory:

> The essence of both transitional experiencing and the transition into object usage is the heady and wonderful world of creative experiencing wherein self and other have the opportunity to become real. Failures in either or both of these developmental currents lead to the development of one or other variety of false self; from the baby's point of view they might well be called failures of faith . . . failure of the transition from object relating to object usage would result from different (but probably related) failure of the caretaker: retaliation, defensiveness, negativity on the part of the caretaker or crumbling of her or his effectiveness. In either case the triple misfortune is that the subjective object never becomes real but remains a bundle of projections, and externality is not discovered; as a corollary the subject is now made to feel that he or she is destructive; and finally, fear and hatred of the other develops, and with them, characterological destructiveness comes into being. In short we have the setting

> for the development of sadism (in what remains a unit self, a self as isolate), the need to aggressively control the other as a perversion of object usage. (p. 117)

Ghent's description of "the need to aggressively control the other as a perversion of object usage" captures the quality of Mr. Brodsky's sadism, and the exploration of transitional spaces such as keeping his cat in the garage, preoccupation with Dr. Abassi's cars, her parking lot, and her walk to the office alone on Saturdays may have signaled efforts to transition into object usage.

The intertwinement of large group identifications with Mr. Brodsky's characterological destructiveness was particularly evident in the material from the day Yasser Arafat and Yitzhak Rabin shook hands: "On the day this news broke, Mr. Brodsky brought it up in the session and then could not speak. We then learned that even though he knew I was from Pakistan, he had not allowed himself to 'know' I was a Muslim."

Salman Akhtar (2014) described the large group identification enacted in this erasure of Dr. Abbasi's religion in "The Mental Pain of Minorities." He defines a minority as a member of a group with weaker social praxis, including lesser political representation and lesser economic clout:

> the majority responds to the minority by ignoring its existence; not seeing becomes tantamount to eliminating or erasing those who seem different and "not like us" . . . this narrow-minded vision of others assaults their complexity and reduces them to cardboard figures. (p. 139)

In the second clinical vignette, Dr. Abbasi is no longer "cool like James Bond." She steps out of a constrained version of her analytic identity with internal dialogue and countertransference experiences that convey the rich interplay of her own internal and external reality with an Indian Hindu patient. Mr. Gupta enacted their shared history of living as minorities in the United States and the long history of prejudice between Muslim Pakistani and Indian Hindu cultures in hateful attacks on Dr. Abbasi's social identity.

Mr. Gupta sought out treatment with Dr. Abbasi while working in the United States and reengaged in treatment by telephone ten years later after moving back to India, shortly after the terrorist attacks in Mumbai in 2008. In a session just before Dr. Abassi was about to take a vacation, Mr. Gupta brought up a Bollywood film, *My Name is Khan* (2010). The movie tells a story of several South East Asian immigrants who come to the United States around the 9/11 event. A Hindu woman turns against her Muslim husband through identification with White American Islamophobia. Mr. Gupta enacted that tableau for the duration of the session, casting himself as the Hindu wife while repeatedly turning against Dr. Abbasi's ethnicity and religion in a series of identifications with large group aggressors.

> "I am wondering how it is for you now in America? Are you being discriminated against? Do people think you might be crazy, like a terrorist? I found myself thinking, the other day, do people even call you to see you for treatment? Or do they feel they don't want to come to you for analysis because you're a Muslim from Pakistan?" Dr. Abbasi responded, "And that would serve me right, wouldn't it? For leaving you." He then spoke at length about travel policies that imposed body scan and search requirements for passengers from Muslim countries, but not for passengers from India, and how those would likely affect Dr. Abassi's upcoming travel plans. He brought up the Mumbai terrorist attacks, with Dr. Abbasi responding that he contacted her shortly after that event to resume treatment. He responded, "Yes, exactly . . . . But what if we disagree about where the terrorists came from? What if I insist that they were Muslims trained in Pakistan, and you don't want to see it that way? It's one thing when you get all animated trying to help me assert myself, but what if you get really angry as we speak about these major issues we might think very differently about? I don't want to piss you off.

Mr. Gupta's attacks remained unrelenting throughout the session despite Dr. Abbasi's repeated interpretations of the intrapsychic conflicts that were being defended against through large group racist identifications. Volkan (2015) has thoroughly described these clinical experiences in which large group identities often serve as a defense against remembering personal traumatic losses and working them through in treatment.

The paucity of psychoanalytic terms available to describe the interplay of intrapsychic and social worlds has led me to use established psychoanalytic terms outside of their usual specified meanings in an effort to convey ideas that have not been well theorized. Akhtar (2013) has provided valuable new terms to expand psychoanalytic theory into the psychosocial domain. His concept of "psychoanalytic anthropology" is apt in describing the theoretical orientation demonstrated in the first two vignettes, in which the recognition of intrapsychic conflicts is privileged over cultural trauma and conflicts. In the third clinical vignette with a white Christian female patient, Dr. Abassi came to frame prejudice as a having a distinct function from its defensive intrapsychic and dyadic functions. Her clinical approach of careful attention to omitted material and the introduction of sociopolitical material is most evident in this last vignette, and seemed to have evolved through a confluence of factors: the intensity of recent sociopolitical events, the clash of worldviews between herself and the specific patient, and the changes in psychoanalytic culture to include psychosocial material as described below by Maxwell Sucharov (2014):

> Just as the original relational turn liberated mental life from the confines of intrapsychic space, a complexity systems view liberates the therapeutic

> experience beyond the confines of the dyadic field. Within this view, social/political context constitutes a continuous and vital presence of the therapeutic process. The expansion of our contextual lens beyond dyad and family to include political and social context can be understood as contextualism in the wide sense, or "radical contextualism." (p. 30)

The first two analytic couples in Dr. Abbasi's paper could be viewed as similar in their social experiences as immigrants from minority religions, and their political orientation to the white Christian majority was also likely to have been similar. The political and social context in those vignettes seemed grounded in a shared liberal, multicultural, multiethnic worldview in which individual social differences were viewed as natural and beneficial to the whole. Social and political differences in reference to the white Christian hegemony were only explicitly developed in the last vignette, as the oppressive aspects of culture came into full relief. Another difference I noted in the third vignette was that the inevitable impact of my own biases as a privileged white American woman became more apparent as I considered the psychosocial elements in the unfolding of the clinical material.

Dr. Abbasi and the previous two patients were professionals with post-secondary education whose successes were not significantly impacted by physical appearance. In contrast, the first thing Dr. Abbasi noted in her paper about Agnes was that she was a beautiful woman. She also noted that Agnes was single until she was in her thirties, yet it seemed doubtful that she had pursued any meaningful career or educational opportunities since the only references to her agency were within the frame of her culture's highly gendered roles of mother and wife. It also seemed unlikely that Agnes had ever been away from her cultural home, or even travelled as a tourist abroad in any impactful way.

Agnes' social identity developed through conformity with American free market capitalist culture and Christian cultural expectations that leverage women to obtain connectedness and value through submission of their agency to others. That cultural message was clearly conveyed by her parents: "I was just forgotten about, I could wait, I was supposed to make do. If I had a sport event, or a performance, and so did they, well guess what, where do you think my parents went? To my brothers,' of course! Because they were younger, and I was older, I was supposed to be reasonable."

Agnes' parochial worldview was echoed in her explanation of why she and her husband were Republicans. She stated that her husband voted Republican because "he likes lower taxes for businesses and the wealthy." Agnes became socially adept at helping her husband expand his business, with both partners thus conforming to their cultural ideal of male self-promotion as a means to furthering privilege.

In addition to voting for Trump as a submission to her mother, "because her mother would be angry if she didn't." Agnes said she always voted for Republicans "because she is Catholic." Catholics are not a united voting block in this country, and her limited knowledge about the history of her religion is conveyed here. Her response probably reflected conformity with the local hegemony of Christian ideology, in which women are valued for their ability to bear children. Agnes' mother upheld that cultural position when she quickly remarried after her divorce, and had four children with him in short order for a total of seven children. In that worldview, women can identify with a sense of omnipotence through submission of their agency to their roles as mothers and wives. Thus, the potential election of a female, pro-choice president undoubtedly posed an existential threat. Agnes was described as a proud homemaker, but the cultural constraint of her role to trophy wife and mother/caretaker must have contributed to the envy she experienced of her husband's success and the sibling rivalry with her brothers.

Agnes' ambivalence around "speaking her mind" carried interwoven strands of psychosocial and developmental difficulties throughout the material. Silencing herself in order to prevent offending others allowed her to conform to cultural expectations and avoid the fear of social devaluation, but left her yearning for expression and acknowledgment of her agency. The submission of her agency also likely reflected a "failure of faith" in the realness of self and others as a legacy of caretaking failures that impeded her development from object relatedness to object usage.

The high level of gratitude and appreciation Agnes expressed to Dr. Abbasi may have been another submission in the service of cultural conformity as well as a manifestation of developmental difficulties. Dr. Abbasi wrote: "She had often said she loved me and felt grateful to me . . . she was with her Muslim analyst, whom she professed had helped her a lot, whom she even professed to love." The feelings Agnes expressed about her analyst may have reflected a transference that was a "bundle of projections" (Ghent) and not an experience of Dr. Abassi as a separate person who had chosen to help her. Agnes' projection of Dr. Abassi as an idealized caretaker perfectly in tune with Agnes' needs would have perpetuated an illusion of omnipotent control over the object/analyst, and precluded either member of the dyad from experiencing shameful or envious feelings in the face of unmet needs.

The developmental and psychosocial difficulties that were being enacted in Agnes' transference first became accessible through Dr. Abbasi's countertransference when Agnes did not mention Trump's win the day after the presidential election. Agnes began that session talking about an experience in which she did not speak her mind, this time recounting an interaction in which she wanted to avoid "offending" a friend. Through processing Agnes' omission of the important event in her own internal dialogue, Dr. Abbasi "spoke her mind" and brought up the presidential election. Agnes responded by becoming visibly tense and said, "I am not talking about the elections. I didn't bring that up. Why are you bringing it up?" Agnes' omission and anxious reaction to material being brought up outside of her area of control cued Dr. Abbasi to the lack of interpersonal connectedness.

The seeming contradiction of someone so culturally insular and compliant choosing an analyst so "foreign" to herself may have signaled a hope for a "new beginning" (Balint, 1968) through the opportunity to "further her recognition of a not-me world, and the establishment of the me" (Winnicott, 1953, p. 89). Thus, Agnes' choice of an analyst from so far away may have indicated a longing to push up against an object who was undoubtedly different in reality from her, an analyst who could more easily be placed outside the area in which her projective mental mechanism operated, outside the area of her omnipotent control (Elkins, 2017).

Dr. Abbasi responded to Agnes' discomfort about her intentions in bringing up the election with reassurance that her patients' well-being was her only motivation: "You suspect my motives. It's hard to imagine I might ask all my patients their thoughts about why they vote the way they do, and what each candidate means to them.' Agnes then responded very brightly, 'Trump always tells it like it is! And I really like that about him. Because, you know, I am just like that: I always speak my mind, even if people don't like it. So for me, that was my big draw to him, that we are both the same in that way.'"

The dramatic shift in Agnes' self and object representations seemed to have been triggered by Dr. Abbasi stepping out of Agnes' area of omnipotent control. Dr. Abbasi's willingness to risk "offending" Agnes by speaking her (autonomous) mind likely brought to Agnes' awareness feelings of shame, envy, and longing that had been split off through enactment of the idealizing transference. The emergence of those split off feelings likely triggered the projective identification onto Trump who she cast as someone who can fearlessly speak his mind because he/she are never affected by other people's minds. The rapid shift to the identification with Trump allowed a continuation of the dyadic projections of an omnipotent subjectively experienced object with the parallel self-experience of being cared for perfectly, thus allowing Agnes to not "care" what Dr. Abassi thought about her vote, because he/she "tell it like it is . . . even if people don't like it."

Dr. Abbasi's interpretation captured the multiple interwoven developmental, cultural, and existential aspects of the transference: "It feels like such a bind for you. To have your own opinion and to express it is to risk losing the love and approval of people you care about. Perhaps including me?" The large group identification in which these intrapsychic and dyadic experiences were invariably embedded was voiced in this passage that revealed the oppressive elements of Agnes' white Christian identification: "I voted for Trump. I can't imagine you did. I am almost sure you wouldn't, given what I know about you. And his views about Muslims, and immigrants." Agnes' shift to the difference in their social praxis would have intensified the experience of Dr. Abassi as "foreign" and as outside the area of her omnipotent control.

Through reflection on that session, Dr. Abbasi became aware that aspects of Agnes' identity had been split off from their relationship: "I found myself feeling, suddenly, a sense of horror, at what I realized had been an ongoing difficulty on my part, about fully appreciating how she compartmentalized, in fact, split off, different feeling states, and pieces of reality." Over the subsequent weeks when they met more frequently, Dr. Abbasi was able to recognize how she had conformed, or colluded, with the enacted aspects of the transference: "a part of me had colluded with a part of my patient, so that despite my intermittent efforts at engaging her in an analysis, I had not been able to do so in the authentic way I do with many other patients." During those weeks, Dr. Abbasi focused on the constraints on Agnes' agency: "I said to her that this was a painful and difficult way to live, the way she was. It took great emotional energy to maintain such divisions in one's mind, and there was, consequently, less emotional availability for immersion in creativity, joy, love, and intimacy." Agnes' response, "as though I'm walking on a tight-rope," suggested the ability to observe herself from Dr. Abbasi's perspective. The emerging externality may have allowed Agnes to also glimpse a constrained future, with its likelihood of decreasing opportunities for recognition as a soon-to-be middle-aged woman whose value was limited to her beauty and attending to her family.

Agnes' increased recognition of herself as an individual, and her subjugation, would have heightened experiences of envy of others free to "speak their mind," but the destructive feelings that were hinted at in the session about the presidential election were not evident in the following weeks and were likely again split off through her culturally conforming characterological submission to idealized powerful caretakers. Jeremy Elkins' (2017) elaboration of the interplay between subject and object in Winnicott's developmental model describes the riskiness to the object/analyst in separation and individuation:

> The establishment of externality "develops naturally out of play with the object" but this is risky play indeed, for what is at stake is nothing less than the expulsion of loved objects from the protection of "the area of . . . omnipotent control" to the desert of "liability not to survive." (p. 131)

Agnes' resumption of the idealizing transference may have been a "regression for the sake of progression" (Balint, 1979) with the submission now carrying the "riskiness" of looming expulsion from the protection of omnipotent control as both Agnes and Dr. Abbasi were becoming increasingly aware of each other as individuals.

Their "play" led to the progression of mutual recognition, while the "riskiness" of that play became evident in the destructiveness of Agnes' omission of the Muslim travel ban. In the face of Dr. Abbasi having made significant efforts to connect more authentically with her, Agnes talked about a dreamy weekend away the day after the attempted Muslim travel ban. During the time that Dr. Abbasi had personally experienced the trauma of the attempted ban, Agnes evoked images of looking beautiful in a bathing suit, frolicking with her (white) family and making love to her (rich) husband. By submitting Dr. Abbasi to the details of her unfettered travel over that fateful weekend, we heard Agnes' "need" for Dr. Abbasi to witness her privilege as a "suitable target for externalization":

> On the other hand, the majority craves for a minority group. The latter serves as a "suitable target for externalization" (Volkan, 1997) of the majority group's paranoid and depressive anxieties. This "need" for a minority group is ubiquitous. In turn, it can lead to an uncanny sense of invisibility on the part of the minority. (Akhtar, 2014, p. 139)

As Dr. Abbasi experienced the enactment more profoundly, the complete destruction of the analytic process seemed at play. Perhaps hoping there was a way back to the recent glimmer of mutuality, Dr. Abbasi brought up the travel ban by wondering if Agnes may have missed the news about the travel ban while she had been away. In a further negation of any connectedness, Agnes again just expressed tense discomfort: "No, why would you think that? Of course I know about that. But I just wanted to tell you what a good weekend I had with Ryan and the family. Should I not talk about that?"

With that response, Agnes pushed Dr. Abbasi completely out of the field of her omnipotent control, into a desert of "not-me" dehumanized others. This time there was no collusion from Dr. Abbasi with reassurances that her only desire was to help her patients. Instead, Dr. Abbasi gave voice to the racism she experienced in Agnes' dismissal of the travel ban as an important issue. Lynne Layton's (2006) conceptualization of the racist field illuminates the enactment:

> Whatever reminds us of our fragmentary nature stirs aggression and narcissistic rage. Splitting and projection may be universal mechanisms of defense, but racism creates the wounds that marshal such defenses, and it is within a racist field that people enact the repetitions that simultaneously keep the wounds fresh and seek to heal them. (p. 250)

The actualization of cultural constraints by the sudden and unpredictable show of force was shocking to everyone in our country, regardless of political ideology. It would have brought with it a heightened awareness for both

Dr. Abbasi and Agnes of their "fragmentary nature." Agnes again shifted to an overt identification with white Christian privilege in the face of seeing her analyst as vulnerable and no longer capable of caring for her exclusively, but in this enactment the reality of cultural oppression in her identification was undeniable. The racist field between them became the arena in which Dr. Abbasi was clearly cast as the constrained minority, an envious witness to Agnes' fantasy of omnipotent privilege in which she and her family were free to travel as they pleased.

> How much better today, to be the one who gets to be all happy and serene , while I and thousands of others like me, are getting "trumped" by Trump. . . . How do I like it now? To be the outsider, to be trumped by you, and others like you, I, the ignored and helpless minority, while you are in control and included in the majority. I think it feels like a useful way, to you, of gaining some control over your feelings about those painful, out of control, humiliating experiences while you were growing up.

In speaking out about the cultural trauma and its effects on her, Dr. Abbasi processed the hateful enactment rather than splitting it off into the earlier co-construction in which her only desire was helping Agnes. Thomas Ogden (2017) conceptualized the process of the mother becoming real to her infant, and the psychological risk to the analyst when that process occurs in treatment:

> The mother also becomes a real external object for the infant in the process of his experiencing the psychological work involved in surviving destruction, a form of work that does not occur in the world of fantasied objects. The analyst or mother may not be able to survive destruction. (p. 1243)

Dr. Abbasi openly worked though feelings of abandonment and denigration by turning to her humanist values to reestablish a sense of meaning and connectedness after Agnes' attack. Dr. Abbasi's unguarded responsiveness allowed Agnes to see her analyst as a unique individual able to repair her sense of meaningfulness and value. Through that process, Dr. Abassi mirrored Agnes as a privileged and accountable woman. Perhaps for the first time, Agnes' may have been able to "use" Dr. Abbasi to feel herself as real, as having been able to hurt her analyst. In that moment, Agnes may have "become an individual" (Slavin, 2010) whose uniqueness was not overshadowed by large group identifications.

Dr. Abassi began her paper by asserting her belief that talking about major sociopolitical events, along with careful attention to the meaning of omitted material in herself and her patients, is necessary. She went on to show how her approach led to recognizing prejudice as a manifestation of intrapsychic and dyadic conflicts in the transference. By the end of the paper, we saw how introducing sociopolitical events revealed the racist field in which intrapsychic, dyadic, and psychosocial conflicts are embedded. Along the way, we witnessed Dr. Abbasi evolve into an analyst who does not replicate the silence of our psychoanalytic forefathers by ignoring the "psychosocial layer within the psyche that contains and secrets crimes of humanity." (Holmes, 2016, p. 642)

Chapter 8

Experience-generated Hostile Destructiveness Fuels Hate, Violence, and Terrorism

A Concluding Commentary

Henri Parens

This 48th Margaret Mahler Symposium undertook the task of shedding further light on that deplorable range of conditions and behaviors in which from time immemorial, individually and collectively, *Homo sapiens* is only too well exercised. Given the horrendous consequences to which these conditions and behaviors have led, it is decidedly in the service of society that we try to further understand what drives them, how to best cope with them, and even how to improve our ability to prevent them from occurring. On this, psychoanalysis can and must speak out on behalf of society. This assertion is not new. In 1933, seventy-seven-year-old Freud came to the remarkable conclusion, one he believed to be "so exceedingly important, so rich in hopes for the future, *perhaps the most important of all the activities of analysis* . . . [which] is the application of psychoanalysis to education, to the upbringing of the next generation" (p. 146; italics added). I have found merit in enlarging this assertion: the application of psychoanalytic knowledge to understanding all matters pertaining to the behaviors of human collectives, especially so, the large-group psychodynamic conflicts that have arisen from their "narcissism of [not so] minor differences" (Freud, 1921, p. 101), including their political and economic philosophies, and all matters arising from their differing ideologies. In this I am in accord with—and coming from a different experiential frame am myself engaged in—what Vamik Volkan has set himself out to achieve, to develop a psychoanalytically informed large-group psychology (Volkan, 2010; also this volume). Let me first turn to what Vamik Volkan brought to this Mahler Symposium, and as he has done so frequently, invited us to leave the familiar frame of the clinical situation and look at the world-wide dread of our day, terrorism.

THOUGHTS ON VAMIK VOLKAN'S "GODS DO NOT NEGOTIATE . . . TERRORISM"

While God—in one conceptualization or another—is part of the majority of humans' lives, there are some for whom looking for God's help is not a solution. With most respectful apologies to Romain Rolland (Freud, 1927) and the majority of our multiethnic world society, Volkan's title brings to mind the rather similar statement I made in 2004: "God cannot prevent Holocausts" (Parens, 2004, p. 192). We can only look to ourselves, to our individual large-groups, to understand how we got into terrorism. Psychoanalyst Volkan who has given much professional time to this question presents us with "a psychohistorical look" at it.

Volkan gives us a rationale for his interest in applying psychoanalytic thought to a "large group psychology *in its own right*." Aware of the much held-to dictum of anonymity on the part of the practicing psychoanalyst, like others among us, Volkan's own life experiences from early childhood on wakened in him an interest to consciously—and most likely unconsciously—revisit and try to understand the experiential factors that so dramatically impacted his own life by subjecting these to psychoanalytic scrutiny.

It is most welcome that Volkan has done so in light of the recently published work by Emily Kuriloff (2014). Kuriloff's study points to the remarkable failure on the part of harshly traumatized European analysts who came to America and became preeminent theorists and teachers of psychoanalysis here who, for reasons both understandable and incomprehensible, did not explore the effects of their own traumatic experiences on their psychoanalytic work, clinical, theoretical, and academic. For complex, still further to be understood, reasons,[1] they remained rigidly loyal and limited to what they had learned about the development and workings of the psyche during the pre–World War II era, as though the threat to life they experienced under the burgeoning Nazi regime that eventually compelled them into exile had left no mark on their own psychic life. In her study, Kuriloff, following on her interviews with Holocaust survivors who had come to America during their early adolescent or younger years well before they became psychoanalysts—for example, Henry Krystal, Anna and Paul Ornstein, as well as myself and others[2]—found that they did realize the impact on them of what they suffered in Nazi Europe and wrote about some of the ways it impacted their work, theoretical and clinical (Krystal, 1968; Ornstein, 2004; Parens, 2004; Kestenberg and Brenner, 1996; Kogan, 1995). I can simply say here that, from very early on in both my research and clinical work, I was persistently attentive to my research subjects' and my patients' traumatic experiences; and in some cases, my attention was directed to the consequences of their trauma, especially early life trauma, on their character formation more than on the influence of the vicissitudes of their psychosexual development and even their attachment history—except of course, in those cases where much of the trauma they experienced came directly from their experiences with their primary-object attachments.

For Volkan, progressively, his interests turned to understanding psychoanalytically the motivations and dynamics of "large groups," the term he coined as the focus of his psychoanalytic research inquiry. Paralleling the psychoanalytic concept of identity as we apply it to individuals, Volkan introduced us to the concept of "large-group identity," "the subjective experience of thousands or millions of people" including within this, their historical relations with other large groups and their shared "chosen traumas and glories." Beyond that, just as the individual child incorporates the ideologies that dictate and govern the large group to which his/her family belongs by means of his/her identifications with his/her parents, so does the collective of individuals that constitute the large group identify with their group's ideologies. Given that individuals of large groups do not share the same family historical narrative, Volkan turned to historians to provide him and his research collaborators with the recorded historical narratives of the large groups they studied.

Doing so, as one might expect—and as I found as well (Parens, 2014)—historians and historical texts provide us with large-group histories much as interviewing our patients, or in the case of children interviewing their parents make available to us the patient's family history with their good and ill fortunes, achievements and failures, joys and traumas. Thus, with the help of information-bearing sources, Volkan and his team pulled together the large group's historical narrative and found their way to understanding how the large group's implementation of terrorism as a strategy for warfare came about.

Volkan puts the emergence of terrorism in the context of warfare that goes back 5000 years. It is remarkable that warfare which, according to Volkan, emerged with the formation of states, was so well organized with large armies against equally large armies, employing established strategies, similar rules, conventions, etc. It leaves one to wonder—have there not always been roaming bands of bandits, etc., between neighboring groups, among interethnic groups that would attack and pillage other groups territories and homes? Be that as it may, how is it that "guerrilla warfare" did not seem to develop until the early half of the twentieth century? And how remarkable that "terrorism" did not occur until the latter half of that same century? It makes sense that these latter forms of "unconventional warfare" occurred: smaller states and groups now seemed to find the courage, audacity, determination to stand up to larger powers. Assuming Volkan's reportage to be right, what gave smaller groups during the twentieth century the daring and determination to get into guerrilla warfare and carry out acts of terrorism against much more powerful larger groups? Of course, the only way for smaller, oppressed, less wealthy groups, or even large groups that for long have been oppressed by smaller but more powerful and wealthier groups—for example, the British colonization of India—would be to rise up and fight but to do so in more covert ways, surprising ways, attacking small segments of larger groups' territories and homes. But what might have given rise to smaller groups' daring during the twentieth century to engage in such—"unconventional warfare?"

In answer, let me put forward a hypothesis. Being neither an historian nor a philosopher, I speak as a psychoanalyst committed to the application of analytic concepts to serious social problems. Furthermore, taking my cue from (but paraphrasing) aging Freud's 1925 position, that "the time before me is limited . . . if I see something" (p. 249) worthy of consideration but in no position at this time to do the required study of historical and philosophical texts in support of my hypothesis, I feel it wiser to state it now, and let psychoanalytic colleagues (myself included) who consider it sufficiently meritorious to in time take up the work of gathering supporting information for it, or to discard it along with the many that have met the same fate in the course of the history of disciplined inquiry. The limited but nonetheless striking information I did gather in my attempts to document and propose that *War is Not Inevitable* (Parens, 2014) and to reason what in fact may be a more heuristically valued set of explanations for war's civilization-long history, leads me to the hypothesis I shall put forward below.

My time being limited, I lean on what is acknowledged to not be the most scholarly sources of information—encyclopedias—but may nonetheless, in my opinion, not be much less credible than many a published text written by individual(s) convinced of his/her/their own subjective point of view—not uncommon in many a secondary (textbooks, commentaries) history and philosophical text.

As knowledge has expanded and brilliant humans have built on the brilliance of those who preceded them, despite set-backs caused by overreaching hyper-narcissism of one large group over another, evidence for which—the Crusades, for instance—goes back centuries if not to the beginnings of civilization, the *Enlightenment* according to *Britannica*[3] and *Wikipedia*[4] brought with it:

> an elite cultural movement . . . in 18th century Europe that sought to mobilize the power of reason, in order to reform society and advance knowledge. It promoted science and intellectual interchange and opposed superstition, intolerance and abuses of church and state. Originating about 1650–1700, it was sparked by philosophers Baruch Spinoza (1632–1677), John Locke (1632–1704), Pierre Bayle (1647–1706), mathematician Isaac Newton (1643–1727), and [among still others] historian Voltaire (1694–1778)[5]

The *Britannica* speaks of it as:

> a European intellectual movement of the 17th and 18th centuries in which ideas concerning God, reason, nature, and humanity were synthesized into a worldview that gained wide assent in the West and that instigated revolutionary developments in art, philosophy, and politics. Central to Enlightenment thought were *the use and celebration of reason, the power by which humans understand the universe and improve their own condition.* The goals of rational humanity were considered to be knowledge, freedom, and happiness[6]

We should note that

> these ideas much influenced Benjamin Franklin, Thomas Jefferson and others and that the Enlightenment . . . played a major role in the American Revolution, [that the political ideals it enunciated influenced among other national governing principles] the American Declaration of Independence, the United States Bill of Rights [and] the French Declaration of the Rights of Man and the Citizen[7]

Locke's 1689 *Second Treatise* outlines his ideas "for a more civilized society based on 'natural rights' and 'contract theory'" (wikipedia.org) goes to the point I want to make. According to the *Britannica*, in his

> "social contract" . . . Locke's definition of political power has a . . . moral dimension. It is a "right" of making laws and enforcing them for "the public good." Power for Locke never simply means "capacity" but always "morally sanctioned capacity." Morality pervades the whole arrangement of society, and it is this fact . . . that makes society legitimate[8]

And here is the point I most draw to the reader's attention:

> Locke's account of political society is based on a hypothetical consideration of the human condition before the beginning of communal life. In this "state of nature," humans are entirely free. But this freedom is not a state of complete license, because it is set within the bounds of the law of nature. It is a state of equality, which is itself a central element of Locke's account. . . . Each person is naturally free and equal under the law of nature, subject only to the will of "the infinitely wise Maker." . . . It is a primary function of society to set up the framework in which legitimate contracts, freely entered into, may be enforced, a state of affairs much more difficult to guarantee in the state of nature and outside civil society.[9]

Note as well the then highly advanced ideas put forward by Baruch Spinoza (1632–1677) "democracy; racial and sexual equality; individual liberty of lifestyle; full freedom of thought, expression, and the press; eradication of religious authority from the legislative process and education; full separation of church and state" (*Wikipedia*). Consider the social implications of Locke's and Spinoza's then new ideas.

And considering as well, after the disastrous massacre of 11 million Jews, Russian prisoners of war, Roma (Gypsies), Seventh Day Adventists, and others, during the Nazi era in Europe followed by the Nuremberg Trials of 1945–46, that the world, through its largest than ever assembly of 196 nations, the United Nations, in 1948 came to that most remarkable of resolution, the Universalization of Human Rights—a cause well-celebrated by Eleanor Roosevelt, one of its strongest proponents. Let me also just note in passing that the Women's Liberation Movement born in the 1960s after more than 50 years in the making (starting with the Suffragettes in the late 1800s), and the civil rights movements of African-Americans that mushroomed in the 1950s–1970s, both soon followed the UN 1948 Universalization of Human Rights. A coincidence? I don't think so!

Hypothesis: The largest ever body of nations, the UN, in 1948 declaring that all humans have equal rights, and therefore that every group being constituted of a collective of human beings has equal rights to its existence, has not been lost on humans everywhere. Might this not have psychologically revived and heighted oppressed people's healthy narcissism and emboldened and psychologically fortified many an oppressed large group to exert physical force to assert its members' equal human rights and the right to autonomous self-governance? Given this then, how can a small group demand recognition of its rights when, in the course of their history these have been crushed—for example, the Crusades—and today are again being denied them by the same and again much more powerful group? This confronts the smaller group with the healthy narcissistic need to claim this right, if even by force. But how against a larger group with a massive military force? By surreptitious, surprising, hit-and-run strategies, by "guerrilla warfare" and by "terroristic attacks." What other course of action do they have?

Some brilliant/desperate warrior thought of guerrilla warfare; another of "terrorism." And that was later supplemented by the yet most monstrous human invention, using kids as weapons, as suicide bombers. Volkan is correct, the Kamikaze of World War II were grown fighters willing to die bravely for their large group; they were not deceived kids, lied to with what is written in the Koran, by promises of greatness and supreme gratification after life. In this, where is the line of morality drawn? What can psychoanalysis put forward toward solving, or at least reducing such human miscarriages of adult behavior toward children?

Volkan's conceptualizing that "chosen traumas" and "chosen glories" are strong identifiers of every large group's identity, identifiers that are critical sign-posts of any group's "historical narrative" (Akhtar, 1997), stands as a cardinal explanatory construct for the central cause of large group conflicts. Volkan's detailing the "rather 'hidden'" aspects of history and their psychological impact in expanding Islamic fundamentalism and the evolution of Al-Qaeda and ISIS is a most welcome elucidation of the historical generators of conflict between the West and the Islamic world. Among the central factors that contribute to large-group conflict, Volkan's emphasis on the deceptions put into action on both sides of the conflict highlights one of the very problematic elements in the instigation and perpetuation of conflict between groups. I have identified this problem as the "'group-narcissistic skew': heightening 'self-valuing' attitudes for group members, and commensurately heightening 'other-devaluating' attitudes for the members of the other group" (Parens, 2014, p. 71). There can be little doubt that a central underlying contributing dynamic is the action of a more powerful group on a weaker one, a large group driven by its inflated narcissism imposing its will on a less powerful vulnerable one. Seeing this going on in 1979 Afghanistan, the United States, in its "Green Belt Strategy," increased its investments in Islam in the countries threatened to be brought under the influence of the Soviet Union, hoping thereby to support Islam's efforts to at least neutralize and undermine the Soviet Empire's influence. Matters of course, got increasingly more complicated.

The point I want to make here is that often buried in the complexity of what is embedded in and motivates large-group conflicts, lies not only layers of current threats, pressures to retaliate for past traumas, but in the play of large groups' hyper-narcissistic ambitions at the expense of their neighbors—which nowadays may mean "neighbors" with large areas of land or sea between them. With regard to the rise of Islamic fundamentalism and the "search for a 'Caliph,'" two points stand out: (1) the long existing cold war between two very large powers whose hyper-narcissistic ambitions and reciprocal threats to forcibly have the upper hand over the other are being exercised in areas of common interest, that is, the United States and the old Soviet Union-now-Russia being played out in the Middle East; and (2) the cyclicity of hyper-narcissism and narcissistic injury between the West and Islam, a chosen glory for one and simultaneous chosen trauma for the other. There can be little doubt that the Crusades of one thousand years ago in which hundreds of thousands of Muslims were slaughtered by Christians in the latter's efforts to "reconquer" the land where Christianity, like Judaism and Islam, were born at the very least contributed to ISIS' battle with the West, and with it gave rise to acts of terrorism that now plague the West. Consider Ryan Lucas' report on National Public Radio, February 24, over one year ago, that "The Islamic State group's online radio . . . said . . . that IS fighters had detained 'tens of crusaders' . . . IS frequently refers to Christians as 'Christian crusaders'" (Lucas, 2015).[10]

I have drawn attention to "The Cyclicity of Hyper-Narcissism and Narcissistic Injury." Both *hyper-narcissism* and *narcissistic injury* create reactivity in groups that mushroom into conflict and even war. Clearly *hostile hyper-narcissism*, but specifically *malignant hyper-narcissism* commonly activates the "group-narcissistic skew" (e.g., "we are far better than them!"). In the course of history, this hyper-narcissistic skew has given the hyper-narcissistic group motive-power to harm, even to destroy the other. But not as visible is the fact that *narcissistic injury*, too, tends to generate its own reactive "group-narcissistic skew" (e.g., "we the good; they the bad—those who oppressed and tried to destroy us"). In time, the narcissistically injured group has often retaliated in uprisings, even in revolutions and wars. Thus, chosen traumas are unavoidably the eventual generator of the perpetuation of conflict between the trauma perpetrator and the traumatized large group (Parens, 2014).

In discussing suicide bombers, Volkan tells us of his visit to the Palestinian orphanage in Tunisia where he interviewed five children who had been in Palestinian refugee camps in West Beirut that were attacked by the Israeli Defense Forces in which civilians were indiscriminately killed. He noted that when they were together, this groups of five kids seemed to function quite normally. But when he interviewed them individually, each one of them manifested serious abnormal behavior. Together, they functioned well; individually, they lost the integrity of their sense of self and fell apart. Interestingly, this kind of phenomenon was also reported decades ago by Bruno Bettelheim (1980) who, when he was in Israel, had studied soldiers in the Israeli military. He learned that among the soldiers reared in Kibbutzim, together they functioned quite well in combat situations; but when they were alone, they were often unable to do what they needed to do to fight and/or to save themselves. I have often wondered if being reared in a cohesive group rather than within individual families created high levels of insecurity in them when they are alone, leading me to wonder if they did not achieve a secure level of individuation, and therewith, have an insecure core self-identity formation.

With this, I would endorse Volkan's proposing that where individuation and core self-identity are insecure, the replacement of "a person's individual identity with a 'team' identity" (Volkan, "Suicide Bombers" section) would bring greater security to the individual by virtue of his/her in fact being a member of a group. And we know, as Freud (1921) pointed out, that the individual yielding his/her core self-identity as well as his/her individual superego to the large-group identity, including the group's superego, ideologies, etc., is expectable and common, especially so when a chosen trauma is remembered or activated, or a chosen glory is commemorated or celebrated.

In addition, Volkan's drawing a parallel with German children reared during the Nazi era, addressing Joanna Harrer's Nazi regime-recommended parenting training books, especially her *The German Mother and her First*

Child (Die deutsche Mutter und ihr erstes Kind) (1934), whose essence recommended that children's emotional needs be denied, discipline be harsh and punitive. As I (2011) noted, "Psychological and anthropological studies have documented that harsh authoritarian child-rearing correlates strongly with these children becoming unduly hostile, and hating and destructive over time. German psychoanalysts (e.g., L. Koehler [personal communications] and W. Bohleber [1995]) have said and written that for some generations in Germany, it was believed that in order to achieve unfailing obedience from them, children's will—their *sense of self* and of *autonomy*—was to be 'crushed'" (p. 87).

According to Brisch (2014) "There was a tradition in Germany of what educator Katharina Rutschky termed *black pedagogy,* which was based on child-rearing principles of obedience to authority, strict discipline (including corporal punishment), and self-abnegation. Rutschky (2001) traced this tendency back *to writings on child-rearing as far back as the late 1600s . . .* .The Nazis were able to make use of this educational tradition of unquestioning obedience in their rise to power and their campaign of terror and domination" (Brisch, 2014, pp. 203–204; italics added) (Parens 2014, pp. 227–228). In other words, the child-rearing practices recommended by the Nazi regime had their origins at least three centuries before the Nazis ruled Germany and much of Western Europe. And in this case again, might not the harsh rearing among Germans over a period of three to four centuries that featured the crushing of the child's will, dragging with it his/her sense of autonomy and sense of self, also have heightened the primacy in them of their large-group identity over their individual core self-identity? It was certainly highly visible during the Nazi era.

But coming back to suicide bombers, like adolescents and young adults who have joined radical Islamists and carried out acts of terror, some come from quite well-to-do families—although in my discussions with German analyst M. Leuzinger-Bohleber, who is working with migrant families and has worked with several such adolescents, I find that their parents, some prosperous professionals, have left their children to be reared by hired help and these children then withdrew from their parents, though there is a chance that they felt neglected and even maltreated. I wonder if, considering Chris Hedges' thesis, "War . . . gives us Meaning" (2002) whether some such adolescents and young adults are driven to terrorism pressured by the accumulated hostile destructiveness generated in them by neglect and emotional deprivation from early childhood on, and who up to then have been unable to create meaning in their life?

In my own work, I have dwelled for some time on what Volkan refers to as the "Who Are We Now" civilization. While in accord with him, I come to the issue from a slightly different path. The recent elections in the United States and France, as well as the UK's Brexit, have generated much concern among many of us in the Western world. Two factors lay at the core of this concern: (1) the mounting level of unemployment in many Western world countries—we don't get much information in the West of the status of unemployment in the rest of the world, and (2) the Middle East upheaval, in good measure associated with the West's incursions there, by the Soviet Union/Russia and by the United States and its Allies coalition; by the "past" war in Iraq with its ongoing and evolving conflagration between Shia and Sunni; by the emergence of ISIS on the heels of still alive but quieter Al-Qaeda; the civil war in Syria, and the masses of migrants in search of asylum and the continuation of their life in the West and elsewhere.

In a word: *first*, it is clear that unemployment brings with it much insecurity, distress, even agony, all increasingly intensely psychically painful and the generators of high-level hostile destructiveness and rage. Late 1920–1930s Germany saw masses of unemployed in misery who eventually turned to Hitler, who promised each one of them a Volkswagen; in recent months in the United States, many turned to Trump, who promised them a return of jobs that were no longer available to them. Disregarding the causes for the current rising unemployment, many embraced the rather reckless promises made by the now president of the United States. The fact is that the changes in industry in reaction to the threats that come with global warming and efforts to reduce climate change by reducing our reliance on coal and carbon fuels are insufficient to allay the rage experienced by those impacted by the necessary steps taken by these industries to counter or even reverse climate change. So too, robotization in making machines and the digitalization of human services that are major job eliminators will surely not be reversed despite the cost of jobs for the white working class and African-Americans who were a major factor in the outcome of the recent presidential campaign. Of course this also impacts many late adolescents and young adults who cannot get jobs for the same reasons. There is little question that society must develop educational programs not only to prepare kids for their future employment but also to re-educate, even at a higher pace than is currently done, those whose jobs will not return. The psychological cost to both individual human beings and to society in general of so much pain and malcontentment has already caused much political upheaval and threatens to reverse some of the gains civilization made during the twentieth century; for example, in the 1948 UN declaring the Universalization of Human Rights. Sufficient psychic pain, the sufficient arousal of hostile destructiveness and rage in masses of humans whose plight is ignored by the better-off, as history had taught us can bring about massive reactions that have led to large-group rebellions and revolutions.

Second, the problems caused by the massive migrations from the war-devastated Middle East and the turmoil in North Africa and South America, including the dangers of getting to areas of safety, of finding asylum in other than just refugee camps, and all that follows from these, now further compounded by immigrants being blamed for problems that exist in the land to which they want to migrate for which, as is reasonably asserted, they cannot be held responsible. Yet, once the oppressed in the country to which these refugees migrate have found a rationalized blame-object, namely the refugees, disastrous measure may be taken against these refugees as well as those hoping to migrate to more prosperous lands, despite their innocence in the face of the accusations levelled against them. For instance, the fact that migrants from countries with large Muslim populations may be banned from entry into countries "because they may bring terrorism with them," is a displacement and blaming-the-Other reaction put forward by oppressed and malignant-prejudice-laden Americans and French. The fact is that this blame is not supported by the evidence; that rather, most terrorist acts have been and are carried out by individuals who are citizens and have already lived in the respective countries for years.

Volkan's reference to Talcott Parsons' (1967) "Modernization Theory" points to possible directions in which civilization will evolve, but the jury is not yet out on how far the three expectations to which Volkan draws our attention will achieve their end. I certainly am not in accord with Harle's (2000) view that, in Volkan's words, "Modernization . . . would destroy ethnic identities as ethnic groups become assimilated into larger societies" (last section of Volkan's chapter).

The idea that ethnic identities would be destroyed, considered through the lens of psychoanalysis is not possible. Ethnic identities evolve, but their basic core retains its origins. If we follow what we have learned so far from the more than 5000-year history of civilization, the core of any large-group identity, formed and evolving by virtue of its continuing historical narrative, its established and yet to occur chosen traumas (especially) and chosen glories, will remain. Jews have annually commemorated their enslavement in Egypt over 4000 years ago and celebrated their exodus from it now for as many years; and there is no question that the twentieth-century Holocaust which is now and will henceforth be commemorated annually by them will now also continue to do so. Christians who have now celebrate the birth of Christ and his crucifixion for over 2000 years will undoubtedly continue to do so. And Muslims who have celebrated the coming of the Prophet Mohammad for some 1600 years will also no doubt continue to do so for the foreseeable future; and as ISIS is now reminding the West by decapitating "Christian Crusaders" in the Middle East, they will from time to time commemorate in one form or another, the massacres perpetrated on them during the Christian Crusades of 1000 years ago.

Even more difficult to destroy, the more specific individual core self-identity, which starts from about six to twelve weeks of neonatal life on, and in parallel with attachment compelled identifications with their primary caregivers, the representatives of society to the child (Freud, 1939), will lead the child to bear the stamp "Made in the X, Y, Z Family" (Parens, 2007, p. 24), a stamp that can further develop and evolve *but is at its core indelible.* These identities are all embedded in the ethnicity of the self's given identity.

While ethnicity-specific humans migrate from one country to another, the United States being a prime model of such aggregation of ethnic groups, aggregations of such ethnic groups have dramatically multiplied during the twentieth century and are likely to continue. Indeed, a striking, remarkable phenomenon is taking place. In many urban areas especially, but in some rural areas as well, many children and teenagers have friends and classmates of variable ethnic origins. Many a Christian youth and young adult has friends that are African-American, Japanese, Hispanic, Chinese, Jewish, Muslim, in singles or multiples. Most like each other, know each other, impact each other, argue with each other, develop enmities, even marry each other, etc. The reciprocal acceptance among children, teenager, and young adult collectives of varying ethnic origins overrides the ethnic differences among them. While some mutual adoption of behaviors and character traits occur due to more or less transient inter-identifications among them, what happens there is a substantial degree of acceptance of the Other, all with awareness of their core ethnic differences. But in most cases, this will not "destroy" the core self-identity of these various multiethnic groups of teenagers and young adults. They are teaching all of us a large lesson: reciprocal respect, friendship, affection, cooperation, and collaboration, even inter-marriage. Their ethnicity is informed, not destroyed, by the Others.

I agree with Volkan that regrettably, "the globalization of 'Who are we now?' [, in our day] often manifests as a return to extreme right-wing conservatism . . . [And that] utilizing chosen traumas and chosen glories for increasing large-group narcissism and conservatism is not dangerous by itself. But its exaggeration and contamination with malignant prejudice against the Other or racism certainly creates severe problems" (see chapter 4). And that's where the problem lies.

COMMENTS ON KERRY NOVICK'S "LEARNING ABOUT THE DIFFERENCE BETWEEN HATE AND VIOLENCE"

In addressing this challenge, Novick asks a series of critical questions. First, "How can children learn to know their feelings of anger, resentment, rage, rivalry, suspicion, and hate?" Then she asks, "how do [they] . . . know what to do with them . . . and decide when to act on their feelings or not?" This is followed by "How do we learn the difference between feelings and actions?

. . . [And] what transforms . . . a state of anger into an internal signal?" And finally, she asks, "What modulates the line from helplessness to anger to rage to hate?"

Novick follows this with the following scenario:
"Two teenaged boys videotaped themselves.
One said, "If you could see all the anger I've stored over the past four years"
The other: "More rage. More rage. Keep building it on."

The first: "Except for [my] parents, [my] extended family treated [me] like the runt of the litter. You made me what I am. You added to the rage. As far back as the Foothill Day Care Center, [I] hated the stuck-up kids who hated [me]. Being shy didn't help. I'm going to kill you all. You've been giving us shit for years" (*Time* magazine, December 20, 1999, p. 44; *New York Times*, December 14, 1999). According to Novick, these words are credited to Eric Harris and Dylan Klebold, the boys who killed their classmates and themselves at Columbine High School, now almost 20 years ago.

These lines, Novick's questions, and the above dialogue-scenario she presents, are of profound relevance to our concerns. First, these bring forth the critical matter of considering the impact of *experience* on psychic life, that too often bypassed or ignored other part of Freud's "complemental series" that contribute centrally to co-create the child's evolving psychic development, intrapsychic conflicts, and character formation—and as Abbasi emphasized in her presentation (see below), even impact how we work in the clinical situation given how experience affects both our patients and ourselves—the complementary effects of "inborn endowment and experience," the more cogent variant of the complementary effects of "nature and nurture." Yes, as analysts we consider "the inner worlds of children, adolescents and adults . . . and the developmental [and adaptive] challenges facing children [and adults] as they grapple with both, impulses from within and influences from without" (see chapter 2).

Novick makes her case by presenting us the case of Eddie and his teenaged mother, Sandra, a much abused and traumatized mother who unavoidably brings her own posttraumatic disordered behavior, adaptive struggles, and character to bear on her child-rearing. Novick details how Sandra mingled her tender care of her baby boy with derisive, malevolent names and derogatory characteristics, "Greedy pig" and "You're bad," making him, Novick tells us, the repository of Sandra's own bad feelings. And in his toddler-era magnificent new-world-explorations[11] as well as in her interactions with him, his mother "interrupted every . . . sequence as soon as Eddie showed signs of excitement and involvement." This dynamic, driven by Sandra's problematic attributions of her own impulses to her child, by disrupting the exploratory joys of discovery of the child's new world into which he was recently born, leads among other things to that mother's thwarting Eddie's emerging sense of self and autonomy. Given that the thrust to autonomy is a major contributor to the child's developing sense of self, thwarting that sense of autonomy unavoidably causes the child much frustration that often escalates to (psychic-pain-generated) hostility toward his mother. This in turn imposes on him challenges to all aspects of his efforts to adapt to his new world, to develop his sense of autonomy and self, as well as to his attachment and relatedness to her—the eventual paradigm for his future object relations. Following this pathogenic pattern of relatedness, where many an interaction tends to rouse hostility in the child toward his primary love-object, the direct inheritance of the dynamics of this primary relationship could well promise a future of maladaptation, of large loads of internalized hostility and hate, poor object relatedness and all kinds of hurtful derivatives that Eddie could generate from these.

Critical is Novick's observation that "It was actually Sandra who had trouble staying in control of her own impulses," and Novick describes how playing catch with Eddie when he was one-year-old, Sandra "accidently" hit Eddie's head which she then followed by "playfully" bouncing the ball off his head, calling him derogatory names. Here then, we learn that Eddie, now bewildered "began to hit himself in the head with both hands." And rightly, putting it in my own words, Novick proposes that by both Sandra's "assigning her own anger" to her son and thwarting his exploration-fostered developing sense of autonomy, effectance, and sense of self, Eddie's hostile aggression mounted, evolved into hostile destructiveness which both, accumulated within him and led to his displacing these hostile destructive feelings—no doubt at time in the form of rage—onto other children and even directly toward his mother by calculatedly avoiding eye contact with her when they sat together for a snack. Novick emphasizes that the mother's own traumatic life and the load of hostile destructiveness that accumulated in her as part of her character formation, "being the most important component of [her] child's environment in his early years, . . . had a powerful impact on the early formation of" Eddie's personality (see chapter 2).

Novick then tells us that "If the outside world is overwhelming or terrifying, neglectful or assaultive, babies feel helpless." Here I diverge from the Novicks' assumptions and propose a different line of explanation in response to Novick's starting questions: "How can children learn to know their feelings of anger, resentment, rage, rivalry, suspicion, and hate? [and how do they] . . . know what to do with them, and decide when to act on their feelings or not? . . . How do we learn the difference between feelings and actions? . . . [And] what transforms . . . a state of anger into an internal signal?" And finally she asked, "What modulates the line from helplessness to anger to rage to hate?" (see chapter 2)

My research has taken me on a different explanatory path than the one they took. As I have reported extensively over time, our direct observational longitudinal research of ten mothers with their newborns, the findings from which led me to develop the Multi-Trends Theory of Aggression (MTTA) (Parens, 1979, 2011), gives us an explanation of the nature of aggression and the psychodynamics to which it leads that hold answers to the Novicks' questions that are at variance with theirs.

Very briefly, I summarize the MTTA as follows:

Aggression is a biologically generated inner pressure to act upon, control, and master self and environment. Looking at our very young children's manifest aggressive behaviors, we catalogued them into four categories:

a. *Unpleasure-related destructiveness* (rage reaction of infancy);
b. *Nonaffective destructiveness* (feeding activity);
c. *Nondestructive aggression* (innately driven pressured sensori-motor activity); and
d. *Pleasure-related destructiveness* (teasing and taunting activity).

In the leap from data to hypothesis, I propose that there are three trends in aggression:

a. *Hostile aggression/destructiveness* (categories a and d)
b. *Nonaffective destructiveness* (category b), and
c. *Nondestructive aggression* (category c).

Nondestructive aggression and *hostile aggression/destructiveness* are pertinent for our efforts at prevention and treatment; we need not concern ourselves here with nonaffective destructiveness, that is, prey aggression.

Nondestructive aggression is inborn, biologically generated and essential for adaptation; it fuels mastery of self and environment, assertiveness, and goal-achievement.

Hostile aggression (HA) (the overarching trend from annoyance to anger, and on to hostility and to rage).

Hostile destructiveness (HD) (the subtrend of HA, from hostility to hate and rage)

HA, and therefore HD, is not inborn; and it is not biologically activated;

However, the mechanism for the generation of HA (and HD) is inborn; this mechanism is activated by an experience of psychic pain ("unpleasure");

Psychic Pain is required for the generation of HA: "PP→HA";

Excessive Psychic Pain generates HD: "EPP→HD";

Psychic Pain gives to aggression the affective quality characteristic of annoyance to anger, and increasingly Excessive Psychic Pain does so for hostility, hate, and rage.

Most critical: *HA and HD can be moderated or heightened by experience.*

In summary, regarding the Hostile Aggression/Destructive trend, the MTTA proposes that experience is the foremost generator of HA and HD. The overarching hypothesis defining this trend of the MTTA holds that "Psychic pain (experience) generates HD." Underlying this hypothesis is that "irritability of the protoplasm" is the biological basis of "EPP → HD" (Parens, 1979; see below). Thus, the cardinal hypothesis, "excessive psychic pain generates high-level HD": "EPP → HL-HD" informs that, most critically, HD can be moderated, and it can be heightened by experience.

Relying on this theoretical line of thought, I would answer the questions Kerry Novick asks at the outset of her chapter as follows:

"How can children learn to know their feelings of anger, resentment, rage, suspicion, and hate?" Let me start by saying that "when I use the concept hostile aggression, I mean this as an umbrella term, which includes the well-known range of *hostile feelings* that spans varying levels of intensity *from irritability to anger, then to hostility, hate, and rage* and all the increasingly more destructive thoughts and behaviors these feelings give rise to" (Parens, 2011, pp. 41–42; see pp. 41–45 for further detail). However, in addition to varying levels of intensity, not all feelings are equal, if we can put it that way.

Irritability and *rage* are reflex-like; they occur in reaction to any pain, physical, or psychic even from birth on, irritability to mild pain, rage to intense/prolonged pain. I assume that when cognitive capability emerges, ideation comes after the reaction to the feeling experienced has occurred.

Feelings of *anger, hostility* and *hate* are foremost triggered by experiences of pain that are perceived to be knowingly—even if by neglect—and/or intentionally inflicted on the self, no matter the reason, the source, or the perpetrator of the pain[12]. From six months of age on, *anger* and *hostility*—not *hate*—are cognitively grasped, ideated, and registered, however, at an age-expectable very low level of cognition. Note that "basic trust/ mistrust" also organize by about six months (Erikson, 1959). Nonetheless, given that psychic pain is registered in the mind, is experienced, humans do not have to be informed that they hurt; their bodies know it; and therewith, their psyche knows it.

What is "registered in the mind" evolves with maturation of the brain. According to Kagan and Herschkowitz (2005), we can say that from birth on (if not before), feelings—not yet ideated—are first registered in the amygdala and then the hippocampus. The ideation-to-conceptualization gradient of feelings the young child experiences requires connections between the amygdala and the frontal cortex, connections that are first laid down across brain areas from about eighteen months of age on. Some primitive ideation probably takes place given the behavioral evidence observable before then. Hate is a more complexly ideated conceptualized feeling that is experienced from about eighteen months on (McDevitt, 1983; Parens et al, 1995; 2011).

Note that eighteen months is also when the capability to verbally/gesturally say "No" emerges (Spitz, 1965); and Mahler et al. (1975) proposed that the shift from the Practicing to the Rapprochement subphase takes place.

Then Kerry Novick asks, "how do they . . . know what to do with [their feelings], and decide when to act on their feelings or not?" This contains two questions. First, how do they know what to do with them? I have proposed that the MTTA trend *hostile aggression/destructiveness* is based on a biological model of one animal-tissue-cell, be it a unicellular organism or a multi-cellular organism like mammals, etc. While I first postulated this model in 1979 (p. 110), in 2011 I summarized, "as a student of medicine, I assume that when an irritant [or toxin] gets into a one-cell organism, the protoplasm of the cell—which is the largest part of the cell, much like the white of a chicken egg—reacts forcefully to rid the cell of that irritant [toxin] because it threatens the unicellular organism's survival . . . . [In one-cell or multi-cell organisms] by virtue of the irritability of the protoplasm (a fundamental principle in medicine) . . . the (toxic) accumulation of tension in the cell (organism/self) is experienced psychically as "unpleasure." This sensory-triggered reactivity of live matter serves to protect against the destruction of the cell (self) and acts primarily to rid the cell of the noxious tension . . . .The [self-protective biological] force in *this ridding activity,* . . . [in the psychological domain] is 'aggression'" (Parens, 2011, pp. 42–43).

My answer then to the first part of Novick's second question is that, when the infant or young child or adult is subjected to psychic pain, the survival system within the living organism acts to rid the self of that pain and its perpetrator. Children self-preservatively automatically strike out at a pain-producing other; this is a built-in normal "ridding" reaction to being hurt, especially when the hurt is perceived as intentional.

The second part of question #2 is: it is one of the principle tasks of parenting to help the child learn to discharge hostile aggression in ways that are socially acceptable and to not escalate conflict further. For a detailed explanation to parents on how to handle this challenge constructively, for professionals I have put out *Handling Children's Aggression Constructively* (Parens, 2011) and for parents and other nonprofessional caregivers, a more reader-friendly *Taming Aggression in Your Child How to Avoid Raising Bullies, Delinquents or Trouble Makers* (Parens, 2012).

This Novick then follows with several further questions:

"How do we learn the difference between feelings and actions?" This is a critical question given that "the ridding reaction," that is, "hostile aggression" triggered by the experience of psychic pain is built-in, is automatic—and all one needs to do is to observe one- to three-year-old children to confirm this observation. It is one of the crucial tasks of parenting to help their young children learn that one does not automatically hit another kid or Mom when one is upset by the kid or Mom. You tell the other kid, and even Mom, that you're angry with what he/she did and tell him/her to stop! See what happens. If that doesn't work, you ask Mom or Dad to help you deal with such a situation.

Then, Novick asks, and "what transforms . . . a state of anger into an internal signal?" According to the MTTA anger *is* an internal signal: "Johnny just hurt me, didn't you see?" Don't expect your child to say, "Johnny caused me psychic pain!" Hmm, that'll take some years to learn.

And finally Novick asks "What modulates the line from helplessness to anger to rage to hate?" That the infant is helpless is too simple a statement. Yes, the infant is helpless to feed himself and do other things. But the infant is neither helpless to feel rage nor to express it vocally or even physically; it is virtually reflexive. Ask any mother! From about six months on, when someone inflicts the child moderate psychic pain, anger will be automatically felt and expressed, that is, discharged. Hate will have to wait till the child is about eighteen months. Then, it will most likely flow out, and invariably shock a mother: "I hate you!," three-year-old Jane raged at her mother! Shocked, mother automatically and rather timidly responded, "Oh, I know you don't mean that!"—wondering: "does she?"

MIGHT REJECTION AND ABUSE BY ONE'S MOTHER BE THE ULTIMATE TRAUMA?

Novick's report on young Eddie and his teen mother Sandra convincingly documents the abuse and denigration to which she subjected Eddie, her own son who, as does every infant creature, yearned to be treated responsibly and lovingly by her. How the primary caregiver treats the infant is not only registered in the "trust/mistrust" he develops by six months of age, but it also leaves its imprint on what the child will come to predict and expect from future attachment-objects. Its consequences are large. It brings to mind the case of Richie (Parens, 1987) who was thriving until six months of age—documented not only by history but also by remarkable photographs of him at about six months, one of which could have featured in a food advertisement with the caption: "The Prince wants his dinner!" Smiling, engaged, robust, a beautiful sight of a boy! When at fourteen months of age, one of our project mothers brought him with his caregiving great-aunt into our project for help, he looked no more than eight-month-old, morose, profoundly depressed, explosive.

His nearly seventeen-year-old mother had been living with her aunt and her boyfriend when Richie was born. Aunt and boyfriend soon got into conflict with one another. Boyfriend told Richie's young mother that he was moving out; she could come with him or not! She elected to go with him into a small public housing apartment. Within weeks, boyfriend abandoned Mother and Richie. Devastated, Richie's mother became profoundly depressed, found

Richie's usual demands too taxing; he began to cry inconsolably. Unable to tolerate his crying, mother put her infant into the hall. We learned that at eleven months of age, he was brought to the Emergency Room at our hospital with a clothes-iron burn on his back! Judging the injury and both child and Mother's psychological states, Richie was taken into City custody until he was later taken in by his mother's aunt. Two months later, Mrs. Smith (project mother) brought both into our project to see what we thought and would recommend should be done to help this once magnificently developing infant now a profoundly traumatized failure-to-thrive child. The history and the picture were tragic. How do we gauge this kind of trauma? Yes, Richie's trauma was harsher then Eddie's; but both children suffered unbearable pain at the hands of traumatized mothers. Let me juxtapose another sort of trauma to address the question in the title of this passage.

The worldwide Jewish community admonished us as was so powerfully articulated by Primo Levi, in his powerful poem, "*Se questo e un uomo*" ("If this is a man"),[13] which is addressed to the reader—and with which I introduce my Holocaust memoirs—

You who live safe
In your warm houses,
You who find, returning in the evening,
Hot food and friendly faces . . .

and Levi asks the reader to consider "if this is a man . . . [then] if this is a woman" . . . [Inmates in Auschwitz being brutalized and near death] after which he concludes,

Meditate that his came about;
I commend these words to you.
Carve them in your hearts
At home, in the street,
Going to bed, rising;
Repeat them to your children,
Or may your house fall apart,
May illness impede you,
May your children turn their faces from you. (Parens, 2004, p. 1)

Clobbering! I had always intended to write my Holocaust memoirs. Primo Levi's words struck me to the core. On the 60th anniversary of my mother being sent to Auschwitz, where she was exterminated within days, I began to write my memoirs (Parens, 2004). I had long hidden behind the cloak of the psychoanalyst's required anonymity, I gradually realized, to protect myself from having to face this torturous task. I wrote it; and in the process suffered a fulminating nummular eczema which I described in writing the text.

As one might expect, some of my patients read my memoirs. I had come out of the closet; I had to. And now, as their analyst, I felt responsible to address any questions my patients would pose to me arising from what I had to make public. From several of them I heard, "How can I tell you what's upsetting me when you went through what you did?!" I was surprised by that comment. And invariably, these were patients who had suffered extremely painful experiences at the hands of their own families, their mothers in particular. I was struck. Not so, I told more than one of them; your suffering is much greater. My mother loved me; with that, I could do what I did. Interestingly, Henry Krystal and Anna Ornstein, Auschwitz survivors, said the same words, "My mother loved me." I did not know they said that; they did not know that I said it. I told my patients, we were threatened and made to suffer by our enemy! Hitler had no good intentions toward the Jews of Europe! We knew it. Enemies make one another suffer. But one's own mother?! I have dwelled on this issue as my patients confronted me with it in the clinical situation. My patients led me to wonder, and so did Richie, and now Eddie: *Might not being rejected, abused and neglected by one's own mother be the ultimate trauma?* To this day, one very mother-traumatized patient can't believe what I am telling her in this regard.

A WORD ABOUT "OMNIPOTENCE" IN EARLY LIFE

Let me briefly take up one more issue stirred by Kerry Novick's presentation, again an issue I have long thought about. She speaks of young Eddie, and generalizes so for young children's reaction of dealing with painful situations "according to a 'closed system'" of affect regulations. Specifically, Kerry Novick proposes that the young child's "self-esteem is maintained by a magical belief in [having] omnipotent power to control others." To be sure, we all use terms differently at least to some degree; it's unavoidable.

There is nothing particularly remarkable about psychoanalytic colleagues disagreeing with one another on both definitions of terms and/or concepts they or others have put forward. However, I will proceed with my comment because we all know that such disaccord is part of many disciplines and I believe that were we to try to change this human tendency by imposing constraints on all of us, this might harshly stifle creativity and strangle the discipline itself. I am not the first to register this dilemma; I am very sympathetic with Alice when, in *Through the Looking Glass,* (Carroll, 1871) she observes (paraphrasing), "How can you make words mean so many different things?!" It is exactly because I came to recognize that when a colleague or supervisee especially would say "this patient is really aggressive" I would invariably ask, "What do you mean, specify, please." What do *you* (reader) mean when you say "aggressive?" And when in our mother-infant project I saw the various types of "aggression" evident from neonatal life on, I was compelled to nitpick and break "aggression" down and spell out what I considered the four categories we might agree on have to do with "aggression" and from there, I conceptualize its three trends (see above).

With this, then, I note that Kerry Novick uses the term "omnipotence" when she proposes that the young child's "self-esteem is maintained by a magical belief in omnipotent power to control others" which I believe may not represent what is going on. My question about this statement is that I believe the young child, whose reality testing function is still to be developed, cannot be said to believe himself or delude himself to be "omnipotent." This is because I define "omnipotence" as a conviction on the part of an individual whose reality testing is age-appropriately developed and functioning, that by his powers he can overcome what others can't. This then is the result of over-inflated secondary narcissism (Parens, 2014). And I propose that when a young child's reality testing is yet in the process of developing, a process which I assume begins from about twelve to eighteen months of age on, knowing what he can do and what he cannot do is yet to be discovered. If he acts as Mahler et al. (1975) proposed of the nine- to about eighteen-month-old (practicing subphase) child, as if "the world is his oyster," it is fueled by his primary narcissism that is not yet informed by reality testing.

My point in making this comment is twofold; (1) I am in strong disagreement with colleagues who speak or conceptualize child development along pathological lines. Both M. Mahler and M. Klein did so. Mahler et al. (1975) proposed that the first subphase of separation-individuation theory is the "autistic phase," a label which Marjorie Harley and Anne Marie Weil, and I independently, urged her to change on the basis of observable evidence (Parens, 2016). I proposed that it be labeled "the primary narcissistic phase." Mahler was in accord but never got to the point of making the change. So too, I find problematic M. Klein's (1940) speaking of the early life "paranoid-schizoid" position, which derives from her conviction of the inborn death instinct basis of aggression. Both are pathology-based concepts that I firmly hold do not describe normal child development. The second part of my objection to murky references of what is normal child behavior comes from the fact that quite commonly, when an adult is behaving in an obnoxious way, it is often said of him/her that "he/she is just acting like a child!" I protest. Of course, children may at times act in obnoxious ways; but when they are behaving in an average-expectable way, they do not act like adults who are acting obnoxiously! Adults who act in obnoxious ways do not act like children; they are acting like obnoxious adults!

The long and short of my diversion is that, with all due respect for my good colleagues, I would say that children under the age of two years do not act omnipotently. They have not yet learned the limits of what they can do in large measure because their reality testing is not yet operative; they operate on the basis of their still intact enough primary narcissism or on the basis of their reactive hostile destructiveness. They soon enough learn that their primary-narcissism-construed-sense-of-self is far more limited than they wish it to be.

Closing this part of my comments, my differing with the Novicks' intrapsychic psychoanalytic explanations that take young children from hostility, to hate and violence does not take away from my accord with their four-point conclusion about what we mental health educators must do. Quite the contrary, I too have been working for five decades toward these same goals.

The Impact of "Major Sociopolitical Events" on the Working Psychoanalytic Clinician

Taking on a large challenge, Aisha Abbasi addressed at least four major issues:

1. The impact on patients and analysts, and therewith on the course of the analytic process, of major sociopolitical events;
2. The question of the feasibility of carrying out an analytic process when patient and analyst come from substantially different ethnic, racial, and/or religious groups;
3. The impact on the patient, analyst, and the analytic process when the groups that give rise to their respective large-group identity are hammered by one (or more) sociopolitical event(s) that puts their respective groups in serious conflict with one another; and,
4. The analytic challenge that comes with the emergence of "Hateful Feelings in the Transference and Countertransference."

As Kuriloff (2014) recently reported, the effects of major sociopolitical events on humans and the impact they have on their psychic lives has not been sufficiently taken into consideration by psychoanalysis and, in the clinical setting, by many psychoanalysts. In her study, Kuriloff observed most cogently, that the many European analysts who immigrated to the United States under the Nazi anti-Semitic threats against them during the 1930s, did not enlarge the corpus of psychoanalytic thought with the effects on their psychic life of the trauma they suffered. Focusing duly in the early years of psychoanalysis on intrapsychic conflict and its central role in the genesis of neurosis, the more or less large effects of trauma on the human psyche, on humans individually and collectively, were much neglected for too long as psychoanalysis developed into the psychological discipline it has become. Kuriloff's study, in asking essentially, "Why did the early forebears of Psychoanalysis in the

US not bring their traumatic experiences to bear on psychoanalytic theory and practice?" further widened a path already carved by Volkan (this volume) in his decades-long considerations of "large group psychology."

In a sense, Volkan addressed the effects of major sociopolitical events on the evolving of any given large group's identity, an identity shared individually and collectively by the members who constitute any given large group. In the course of the unfolding of each group's historical narratives (Akhtar, 1997; Volkan, 1991, 2010), the importance of major sociopolitical events which give rise to that group's "chosen traumas" and "chosen glories" (Volkan, 1997) became clear. Volkan duly noted that in order to maintain their large-group identity, its members are not to allow, both, chosen traumas and chosen glories to fade away and vanish.

It is therewith unavoidable that when a patient and his or her analyst come from distinctly differing large groups, the identity of each will bring group-specific differences between them. While we analysts rightly assume that humans the world over have quite similar psychobiological needs, we also know that with the passage of time, what constitutes group-specific physical and psychological developmental schedules will modify according to evolving ideological parameters that have and continue to elaborate the specification of the group. We also know that due to *Homo sapiens*' long period of helplessness and dependence, the development of children and youth depend on the vicissitudes of their large-group dictates and principles of family formation, a fact essential to fostering their clustering into large groups.

And with this, in the course of every large group's existence events occur that lead individuals and collectives to interpret these events' causes, effects, and meanings which will lead large groups to conceptualize and adopt the explanatory ideologies that by and large become internalized by most if not all the members of the group. In this long evolving historical process, group members come to accept and commit themselves to what they believe to be true and false. But given that all groups do not experience the same events, and that they explain the events that befall their respective group according to their interpretation of these events, they may come into conflict with one another, as human history has already too long borne out. In consequence, what I consider to be the second issue Abbasi explores follows.

In her discussion, Abbasi asks whether a patient and a psychoanalyst who are members of different ethnic, racial, and/or religious groups can carry out a substantially productive psychoanalysis. She posits: "To understand the individual meanings [such] differences have for the patient, starting from the most superficial and accessible and going toward the deepest underpinnings, is one of the tasks of an analysis. Can such a task be accomplished in the presence of gross and obvious differences between the patient and analyst that preclude a shared understanding of a common racial/cultural/religious/ethnic background?" (see chapter 6)

I take Abbasi's words "in the presence of *gross and obvious differences . . . that preclude a shared understanding . . .*" (see chapter 6) to be critical to the question she is asking. I say this because, as Abbasi of course realizes, within any large group—such as the United States or any other nation—there are subgroups, each of which has more or less substantial specific ideological differences with the other subgroups that are members of the larger group to which they all belong. For example, Christianity consists of Catholics and Protestants, each sect of which is further subdivided, such as: Methodists, Southern Baptists, and Episcopal. The same holds among Jews: Orthodox, Conservative, Reformed, etc. So too, from the Middle East through Asia, some Muslims are Sunni, some are Shia, etc. Furthermore, in the United States, while some discomfort may at times come up in the course of clinical work between an Episcopal patient and a Jewish analyst, for example, both having lived in the United States for long and identify as Americans, such discomforts do not seem to stand in the way of their proceeding quite well to productive psychoanalytic work.

But taking Abbasi's considering "gross and obvious differences" as creating the challenge I believe she has in mind, given the analysis of the three patients she reported to us, her review of the literature speaks directly to not only changes in view on the question of such interethnic/religious/racial/cultural analyzability, but also to world demographic changes that have occurred over the past decades. Abbasi tells us that some sixty years ago, "Oberndorf (1954) . . . wrote that . . . 'transference in its most positive form is most likely to be established and [analyzed] between patient and [analyst] if their psychological biases do not differ too widely' (p. 757)" (see chapter 6). Parenthetically, let's assume that Oberndorf's "most positive form" (1954) means that the patient lends himself/herself productively to the psychoanalytic process.

But Oberndorf's view dating back to more than six decades ago is challenged by at least two facts: (1) as Abbasi reports, by a number of analysts who following Oberndorf, found inter-large-group-identity patient-and-analyst feasible when the analyst lends herself/himself with empathy and flexibility to hearing and understanding the patient's experiences even while the ideologies by which they are determined are at variance with the analyst's, and (2) as I noted above, the striking changes in worldwide demographics resulting from both, people the world over seeking better life opportunities in "more advanced" countries in the West with greater economic and educational opportunities than in their native lands, and more recently due to the very dire and dangerous war-burdened conditions prevailing in the Middle East and North Africa which has sent thousands to seek shelter and survival in the West. In addition, with the expansion of educational opportunity fostered by law-determined universal education to subgroups, for example African-Americans in the United States, despite its insufficiently meeting the goals prescribed by law, large advances have been made by many who for too many shameful decades were prevented from such self-development.

This large second fact, the changes in worldwide demographics, has brought with it critical changes pertinent to the issue on which Abbasi reports to us. In consequence of this second fact, as Abbasi so rightly notes, "the candidate population at psychoanalytic institutes [has notably diversified] and more patients from diversified ethnic backgrounds enter psychoanalytic treatment." I recall clearly among others, a specific point on which I dwelled a couple decades ago in the course of analyzing a professional woman from a country in Asia. Long supportive of Women's Equal Rights, I recall distinctly my initial dismay at her acceptance of being denigrated by her father, brothers, and husband. In my own mind I asked, "Why did her healthy narcissism not lead her to stand up for her right to equal acceptance and respect in her family; did they not recognize her intelligence, perseverance and academic-professional achievement; did she not deserve equal acceptance and respect from them?" I ventured on this path of exploration toward such an interpretation. But I soon self-analytically reflected on the fact that, despite my dismay, her achievements did not override what I consider to be the denigrated status of women in her large group's ideology. I recognized, how in many cultures, Jewish Orthodox included, women are relegated to inferior status, to "balcony" status. Obviously, I did not push my wish to interpret as I might have with a patient of my own culture-background. I did find as time passed, that her own view of herself, then in the United States for many years, evolved as she struggled more consciously with the pain inherent in her native self-identity to adopt a more "Westernized" but still native sense of self.

The long and short of my thinking, insufficiently documented by my brief diversion is that, after five decades of analytic clinical experience, I am in accord with Abbasi. I know that empathic and disciplined analysts can achieve a good analytic process with patients of different ethnicity/culture/race. But this then takes me to my next point, there is more to this issue than just the question of ethnic/religious/racial variability between patient and analyst.

To go more directly to Abbasi's "Impact of Major SocioPolitical Events" on the patient and psychoanalyst and their efforts to achieve a productive psychoanalytic process, we have to add this fact to the "simpler" issue of inter-ethnicity between them. Abbasi's three patients illustrate the added complexity of the issue. It is her intention to present these cases "at points when major socio-political events occurred in the world . . . [which she tells us] . . . allowed for the deepening of the clinical work, leading us to understand aspects of the patient's history . . . and conflicts, in new, unexpected, and meaningful ways" (see chapter 6). Dr. Abbasi, a brown-skinned, Muslim, Pakistani-American woman analyst, who has lived in the United States for thirty years, first presents her analysis of a white Jewish man of European origin. Her second case is a brown-skinned Hindu man of Indian origin. Her third case is a white quite wealthy Christian woman of United States origin who, Abbasi notes, did not vote Democrat as did most of her patients—not a minor issue in our present highly politically polarized country; I assume that Abbasi is a Democrat, as are many among us analysts.

With Mr. Brodsky, the external event in question was "the Israeli-Palestinian peace accord of 1993, trumpeted in newspapers all over the world by images of the historic handshake between Yasser Arafat and Yitzhak Rabin." This brought to the fore Mr. Brodsky's youthful participation as an active member of a political Jewish group who organized and engaged "in many anti-Arab and anti-Muslim rallies. [Indeed,] He had been raised to believe that all Muslims were anti-Semites" (see chapter 6). Clearly, this would have been very challenging for any Muslim analyst, unavoidably rousing in the analyst greater or lesser reaction of rejection of her/his patient, and seriously complicating not only the real patient-doctor relationship but certainly impacting both the transference and the analysts countertransference. How could it not? Candidly, Dr. Abbasi tells us that she reasoned: "What . . . did *I* have to do with that . . . remote war between Muslims and Jews?" And she adds, "It is precisely this lack of internal disturbance on my part . . . that should have alerted me that something was amiss with me." Nearly a decade later came "September 11" and Dr. Abbasi shares with us "How [she] changed as an analyst after 9/11." The conflict between Jews and Muslims, from which she could distance herself some years before, now made itself felt as she was as shaken as were the rest of us in America and elsewhere by the event. But for her, a Muslim American now in America for some fourteen years, 9/11 reached into her psyche as she [recognized her] struggle to sort out alliances and where [she belonged] now and much earlier, in her "childhood struggles—over splits, factions, and divided loyalties. [Her] work now took an unexpected turn" as her patients now brought in "their intense fear, and hatred, of Muslims [even] while turning . . ." (see chapter 6) to her for help with their terror of Muslims. What a challenge for any analyst! This makes the ethnic difference between analyst and patient—even if past historical conflicts existed between their ethnic groups but lay dormant in the present—pale when compared to an enormous conflict being activated in the present. But note especially, the psychological growth I would say in Dr. Abbasi as a human being and as an analyst in the face of her work as a healer of patients now ravaged by her own ethnic group of origin's destruction of the Twin Towers and the many people in them. It resonates, though to a far lesser degree, with the plight of second-generation Germans, including psychoanalysts, who live with the knowledge of what their parents did during World War II.

With her second patient, the Hindu man from India, Dr. Abbasi carried out her analytic work with him on the telephone[14] starting in early 2009. His conscious presentation for why he started his work with Abbasi at that time was the rejection he had experienced by a male co-worker whose love-attention he yearned for and toward whom their respective boss at work showed some preference. He had long struggled with his homosexuality and wanted analytic treatment in the hope of modifying his sexual identity. But then came the November, 2008, Mumbai terrorist attacks by "Muslim terrorists . . . from Pakistan." And Abbasi writes, "I thought that immense terror had been unleashed in Mr. Gupta by the combination of his recent mounting anger about being ignored and excluded and the violence and sadism in the terrorist attacks. Did he feel also that I had excluded/abandoned him ten years ago, when he left America to go back to India?" (see chapter 6). With this beginning of the analysis, the "Mumbai attacks by Muslim terrorists," became a large transference determiner and roused in Dr. Abbasi reactivity that generated in her countertransference burdened with "hateful feelings." Again, the interethnic differential between patient and analyst was substantially complicated by the miserable deadly conflict between their respective ethnic groups. While these conflicts were not new for these neighbor-groups, that such a conflict occurred during Mr. Gupta's analysis made it much more challenging for the analyst who is called upon for help.

Dr. Abbasi's third reported case is striking. The external event, the election of Donald Trump, the threat of and enactment, even if unconstitutional in the United States, of the ban on entry into the United States of a large group on grounds of their religious identity, Muslims, came into the analytic space with a vengeance. Jarred by the patient's seemingly oblivious and un-empathic reaction to its implications for her analyst, her analyst's family and her Muslim community, sharply wounded Dr. Abbasi, who experienced a burst of hate toward her analysand—who had repeatedly claimed to "love" her analyst!

I say "seemingly oblivious and un-empathic reaction" because Dr. Abbasi's directly confronting the patient's rather shocking, unexpected reaction loosened in the patient the character defense she had progressively established to protect herself against the enormous pain she suffered at her mother's lifelong treatment of her. Her mother's total lack of empathy for Agnes, who suffered serious narcissistic injury at her hands, even as Agnes' mother demanded unyielding compliance with her wishes, on top of which this very troubled mother preferred the rest of her brood of sons over her one beautiful daughter. Agnes' long enduring torture led her to suppress all feelings and comply passive aggressively not only with her mother but with her husband as well. Her analyst's pain and rage, which compelled Dr. Abbasi to confront her patient as she did, unleashed her patient's underlying mother-transference rage even while this transference-object herself now felt painfully threatened. Which takes me to the fourth issue presented in Abbasi's chapter.

The fourth issue Dr. Abbasi addresses is the analytic challenge that comes from the emergence in analysis of "hateful feelings in the transference and countertransference." Hateful feelings in patients ubiquitously emerge in analysis. Often, though not always, they become externalized and attached to the analyst who then, as we should as transference-objects, proceed to analyze them. We have all been the recipients of such feelings. My experience is essentially that of an "ego psychologist" who does not hesitate to use the several other models now at our disposal—for example, attachment theory, self-psychology, inter-subjectivity. The emergence of hate feelings toward the patient in the analyst's countertransference, while dealt with highly variably by each of us—not uncommonly eliciting unpleasantness, at times some shame—raises the need to further self-analyze and perhaps feel some reprimand from the analytic powers that be. Dr. Abbasi's candor in reporting her experiences in the face of such challenge warrants our appreciation and respect.

While there is much of the case processes I do not know for all three of Dr. Abbasi's patients, I will tentatively comment on what I do see, and hope that Aisha Abbasi will freely take or leave what I postulate here. The writing clearly indicates that each case was analyzed timewise in the order Abbasi presents them. Given that Abbasi's thesis emphasizes ethnic, religious, and racial variations between patient and analyst, she being the only constant, I describe her patients according to their identity parameters.

Dr. Abbasi was a quite younger Muslim-woman-analyst when she analyzed her Jewish-white-man-patient. In his childhood he was significantly traumatized in consequence of which he became a very angry man. He had experienced much pain at the hands of his mother and I think he now maltreated his wife harshly. He clearly gave evidence of experiencing a hostile transference with his analyst. According to the text I read, I think that young Dr. Abbasi may have been a bit too constantly searching for transference implications and therewith, stung by her patient's raw sadism. I found Dr. Abbasi's interventions to be at times too confrontational and at times edged with some sadism on her part. Her very angry Jewish-white-man-patient tended to react with silence to her verbal-affective interventions. The Israeli-Palestinian, Jewish-Muslim efforts at a Peace Accord roused much quiet rage in her Jewish-white-man-patient, who sharply directed some of his long brewing attacks on Muslim "dogs," which was experienced in the transference roused in his young Muslim analyst's unavoidable angry reactivity against which she later recognized she self-protectively detached herself from; yet her interventions were, I thought, sadism-edged. I should note that the patient stayed in analysis and seemed to benefit from his work with Dr. Abbasi.

Nearly ten years later came 9/11. Abbasi reports candidly the enormous conflict and distress which, as a Muslim Pakistani-American this event caused her (and her family and community). I assume that this "major sociopolitical event," as well as the passage of time and her own growth as a psychoanalyst, brought about greater skill, as it does in all of us, in handling the challenges we encounter in our analytic work. So that by the time she came to analyze her Hindu-Indian-man, she was more "experienced."

The Pakistani Muslim Mumbai attacks again presented a hate and rage stirring sociopolitical event for those on both sides of the attacks. These directly impacted both Hindu-man-patient and his Muslim-woman-analyst. While a number of years later than her analysis of the Jewish-white-man at the time of the Israeli-Palestinian Peace Accord, I again felt that in dealing with her hate toward this very injured, self-denigrating homosexual-conflicted angry man whose transference did not seem so heavily invested with rage as was that of her Jewish patient, that Dr. Abbasi's interventions were at times sharp with an edge of sadism. This patient did not react with silence; quite the contrary, he countered his analyst's interventions, saying in essence that he could see that she certainly could get provoked, get very angry, and be difficult. Despite these moments in their work, the patient continued to work with Dr. Abbasi and I don't doubt that he benefited from their work together. I did wonder at one of the interactions Dr. Abbasi describes, whether her patient truly registered the correctness of her intervention or whether he exhibited some masochistic surrender, backing down and quietly saying that she was on target with her intervention.

Then again just less than ten years later, in our present time, Abbasi is analyzing a Christian-white-beautiful-wealthy-woman and reports on the effects, not only of the election of Donald Trump to the presidency of the United States, but especially to his efforts to impose a ban on the entry of Muslims from selected Middle East countries, a ban that while argued and challenged in courts is nonetheless being acted upon and has roused profound anguish and rage among many in the United States but most particularly among Muslims who, like many of us dread the current president's outrageous campaign promise to (unconstitutionally) ban all Muslims from America, legal challenges notwithstanding. But most rousing of hate in Dr. Abbasi is the fact that her very troubled, tightly characterologically defended patient voted for Trump—because he dared "to tell it like it is" which she claimed, though profoundly inhibited and overly compliantly, never gave evidence of it, that she too, "tells it like it is!"

I found that prior to the intra-analytic explosion to which this external event led, Dr. Abbasi's interventions with and attitude toward this patient seemed to be careful, concerned, even gentle, and warm. I cannot discern the reason for that attitude. Was it further self-analytic work and maturation on the part of the analyst? Was it the analysis of a woman? What I can discern is that Dr. Abbasi's outright very angry confrontation of the patient in the face of her indifference and seeming total lack of empathy toward her threatened analyst seemed to have unlocked the patient's long existing inhibition and repression of her rage toward her mother which now materialized in her transference to her analyst. It is reasonable to ask: would this patient's concretized character defense have yielded to analysis without the intensely affective reaction to her on the part of her analyst? Did it, in the context of the safe patient-doctor relationship give the patient permission and the courage to express *her* own long-repressed feelings of rage and outrage? We might not have all done it the same way; but, I have the distinct impression that there is a very good chance, given the process as described, that the ongoing analysis will yield a notably productive outcome.

NOTES

1. I should note that most Holocaust survivors who eventually wrote about their highly traumatizing experiences did so only many years, decades, after it took place. Anna Ornstein published her memoirs in 2004; Paul Ornstein in 2015; H. Parens in 2004. I was not ready to do so until 1999, more than 50 years after I arrived in America. I think that we were all too traumatized to dive into the pit of unbearable emotions. Despite this delay in writing about the trauma and the losses and pain it wrought, on the reflection that came with the writing of my memoirs, I learned that my research and clinical work were in fact both significantly impacted and informed by it.

2. And I would add to this a list of children of Holocaust survivors like Ira Brenner, Ilany Kogan, and Emily Kuriloff herself.

3. The less-than-ideal sources of information I explored, https://www.britannica.com./print/article/188441; http://britannica.com/event/Enlightenment-European-history https://www.britannica.com/biography/John-Locke.

4. http://en.wikipedia.org/wiki/Enlightenment.

5. http://en.wikipedia.org/wiki/Enlightenment, p. 1.

6. http://britannica.com/ event/ Enlightenment-European-history, p. 1; italics added.

7. http://en.wikipedia.org/wiki/Enlightenment, p. 1; also, britannica.com/biography/John-Locke, Locke's Second Treatise.

8. britannica.com.

9. britannica.com.

10. "IS militants kidnap dozens of Christians in Syria," NPR, Associated Press, 12 noon, February 24, 2015.

11. I would like to point out the obvious magnificent fact, that when an infant is born he/she discovers a world he/she has never seen before, the infant's new world. I put it that way because I think it underlies the remarkable thrust to autonomy evident in that once the infant can crawl, many an infant is into everything—often calling the primary caregiver to start that challenging parenting task, limit-setting—an issue about which I have written since 1979.

12. See Parens 2011, chapter 3, for further details.

13. This is also the original title of his Auschwitz memoirs (Levi, 1958), retitled for the English translation, *Survival in Auschwitz* (Levi, 1996).

14. I too am among those who have done analytic work on the telephone with patients far from Philadelphia.

References

Abbasi, A. (1997). *When worlds collide in the analytic space: Notes from a 'cross-cultural' psychoanalysis*. Presented at the Winter Meetings of the American Psychoanalytic Association, New York.

Abbasi, A. (1998). Speaking the unspeakable. In: *Blacks and Jews on the Couch: Psychoanalytic Reflections on Black-Jewish Conflict*, eds. A. Helmreich and P. Marcus, pp. 133–147. Westport, CT: Praeger, 2008.

Abbasi, A. (2008). "Whose side are you on?": Muslim psychoanalysts treating non-Muslim patients. In: *The Crescent and the Couch: Cross-Currents Between Islam and Psychoanalysis*, ed. S. Akhtar, pp. 335–350. Lanham, MD: Jason Aronson.

Abbasi, A. (2012). "A very dangerous conversation": The patient's internal conflicts elaborated through the use of ethnic and religious differences between analyst and patient. *International Journal of Psychoanalysis* 93: 515–534.

Akhtar, S. (1995). A third individuation: Immigration, identity, and the psychoanalytic process. *Journal of the American Psychoanalytic Association* 43: 1051–1084.

Akhtar, S. (1997). *Hindu-Moslem conflict in India*. Presented to Discussion Group #24: Psychoanalytic Perspectives of Prejudice and Beyond, A. Mahfouz, Chair. Meetings, The American Psychoanalytic Association Meetings, New York, December 17.

Akhtar, S. (2003). Dehumanization: Origins, manifestations, and remedies. In: *Violence or Dialogue?: Psychoanalytic Insights on Terror and Terrorism,* eds. S. Varvin and V.D. Volkan, pp. 131–145. London, UK: International Psychoanalytic Association.

Akhtar, S. (2006). Technical challenges faced by the immigrant psychoanalyst. *Psychoanalytic Quarterly* 75: 21–43.

Akhtar, S. (2013). Psychoanalysis and culture: Freud, Erickson and beyond. In: *Psychoanalysis in Asia: China, India, Japan, South Korea, Taiwan*, eds. A. Gerlach, M.T. Salvio Hooke and S. Varnin, pp. 19–41. London, UK: Karnac Books.

Akhtar, S. (2014). The mental pain of minorities. *British Journal of Psychotherapy* 30: 136–153.

Ali, T. (2001). Former USA policies allowed the Taliban to thrive. *Turkish Daily News*, September 25, p. 16.

Anderson, A., and West, S.G. (2011). Review: Violence against mental health professionals: When the treater becomes the victim. *Clinical Neuroscience* 8: 34–39.

Anderson, J.W., and Winer, J.A. (2003). Introduction. In: *Psychoanalysis and History*, eds. J.A. Winer and J.W. Anderson, pp. 1–4. Hillsdale, NJ: The Analytic Press.

Anderson, P.W. (1972). More is different: Broken symmetry and the nature of the hierarchical structure of science. *Science* 177: 393–396.

Antonius, D., Fuchs, L., Herbert, F. et al. (2010). Psychiatric assessment of aggressive patients: A violent attack on a resident. *American Journal of Psychiatry* 167: 253–259.

Anzieu, D. (1984). *The Group and the Unconscious*. London: Routledge and Kegan Paul.

Appiah, K.A. (2015). Race in the modern world: The problem of the color line. *Foreign Affairs Magazine*, April 7, 2015. *www.foreignaffairs.com*, accessed April 29, 2017.

Bachman, R. (1996). Epidemiology of violence and theft in the workplace. *Occupational Medicine* 11: 237–241.

Bair-Merritt, M.H. (2010). Intimate partner violence. *Pediatric Review* 31: 145–150.

Balint, M. (1979). *The Basic Fault: Therapeutic Aspects of Regression*. London/New York: Tavistock Publications, p. 132.

Balsam, K.F., and Szymanski, D.M. (2005). Relationship quality and domestic violence in women's same-sex relationships: The role of minority stress. *Psychology of Women Quarterly* 29: 258–269.

Banyard, V.L. (2008). Measurement and correlates of pro-social bystander behavior: The case of interpersonal violence. *Violence and Victims* 23: 85–99.

Bard, M., and Sangrey, D. (1986). *The Crime Victim's Book*. New York: Brunner/Mazel.

Basch-Kahre, E. (1984). On difficulties arising in transference and countertransference when analyst and analysand have different socio-cultural backgrounds. *International Review of Psycho-Analysis* 11: 61–67.

Berman, E. (2009). *Radical, Religious, and Violent: The New Economics of Terrorism*. Cambridge, MA: MIT Press.

Bernard, V.W. (1953). Psychoanalysis and members of minority groups. *Journal of the American Psychoanalytic Association* 1: 256–267.

Bettleheim, B. (1980). *Surviving and Other Essays*. New York: Vintage Press.

Bloom, P. (2010). Why we like what we like. *Observer* 23: 3. *www.psychologicalscience.org*, accessed April 29, 2017.

Bohleber, W. (1995). *The children of the perpetrators—the after-effects of National Socialism on the following generations*. Presented in Toronto, May 4, 1995.

Bowker, L.H. (1983). *Beating Wife-Beating*. Lexington, MA: Lexington Books.

Brisch, K.H. (2014). German perspectives on Henri Parens' pioneering work in Philadelphia: The development of attachment-based parenting programs. In: *Early Parenting and The Prevention of Disorder Psychoanalytic Research at Interdisciplinary Frontiers*, eds. R.N. Emde and M. Leuzinger-Bohleber, pp. 203–215. London: Karnac Books.

Brown, C. (2008). Gender-role implications on same-sex intimate partner abuse. *Journal of Family Violence* 23: 457–462.
Browne, A. (1987). *When Battered Women Kill*. New York: Macmillan.
Browne, A., and Williams, K.R. (1989). Exploring the effect of resource availability and the likelihood of female-perpetrated homicides. *Law and Society Review* 23: 75–94.
Brownmiller, S. (1975). *Against our Will: Men, Women and Rape*. New York: Simon and Schuster.
Buchwald, E. (1993). Raising girls for the 21st century. In: *Transforming a Rape Culture,* eds. E. Buchwald, P. Fletcher and M. Roth, pp. 179–200. Minneapolis, MN: Milkweed Editions.
Burn, S M. (2009). A situational model of sexual assault prevention through bystander intervention. *Sex Roles* 60: 779–792.
Caesar, P.L. (1988). Exposure to violence in the families of origin among wife-abusers and maritally nonviolent men. *Violence and Victims* 3: 49–63.
Campbell, B.K., Silver, D., Novick, K.K., Novick, J., Mittlestaedt, M., and Walton, A. (1995). The application of Lichtenberg's five motivational systems to the analysis of mother-infant interaction. *Psychoanalytic Inquiry* 15: 481–492.
Campbell, J., Messing, J., Kub, J., Agnew, J., Fitzgerald, S., Fowler, B., Sheridan, D., Lindauer, C., Deaton, J., and Bolyard, R. (2011). Workplace violence: Prevalence and risk factors in the safe at work study. *Journal of Occupational Health Environment* 53: 82–89.
Campbell, R., Greenson, M.R., Raja, S., and Bybee, D. (2008). The co-occurrence of childhood sexual abuse, adult sexual assault, intimate partner violence, and sexual harassment: A mediational model of posttraumatic stress disorder and physical health outcomes. *Journal of Consulting and Clinical Psychology* 76: 194–207.
Carmel, H., and Hunter, M. (1991). Psychiatrists injured by patient attack. *The Bulletin of the American Academy of Psychiatry and the Law* 19: 309–316.
Carroll, L. (1871). *Through the Looking Glass*. London: Macmillan Press.
Caschetta, A.J. (2015). Does Islam have a role in suicide bombings? *Middle East Quarterly* 22: 1–19.
Chandler, S. (1986). *The Psychology of the Battered Woman*. Unpublished doctoral dissertation. Berkeley, CA: University of California, Berkeley.
Chasseguet-Smirgel, J. (1984). *The Ego Ideal*. New York: W.W. Norton.
Chen, C., Huang, C., Hwang, J., and Chen, C. (2010). The relationship of health-related quality of life to workplace physical violence against nurses by psychiatric patients. *Quality of Life Research* 19: 1155–1161.
Cheney, D.L., and Seaforth, R.M. (2007). *Baboons' Metaphysics: The Evolution of the Social Mind*. Chicago, IL: University of Chicago Press.
Chomsky, N. (2003). *Hegemony or Survival: America's Quest for Global Dominance*. New York: Henry Holt and Company.
Christopoulos, A. (2014). External and internal reality: The impact of the current socio-economic crisis on the analytic dyad. *International Journal of Psychoanalysis* 95: 1131–1153.
Coker, A.L., Smith, P.H., McKeown, R.E., and King, M.J. (2000). Frequency and correlates of intimate partner violence by type: Physical, sexual and psychological battering. *American Journal of Public Health* 90: 553–559.

Connolly, C., Huzurbazar, S., and Routh-McGee, T. (2000). Multiple parties in domestic violence situations and arrest. *Journal of Criminal Justice* 28: 181–188.

Daffern, M., Mayer, M., and Martin, T. (2006). Staff gender ratio and aggression in a forensic psychiatric hospital. *International Journal of Mental Health Nursing* 15: 93–99.

Dalal, F. (2002). *Race, Colour and the Process of Racialization: New Perspectives from Group Analysis, Psychoanalysis and Sociology*. Hove, England: Brunner Routledge.

Dasgupta, S.D. (2002). A framework for understanding women's use of nonlethal violence in intimate heterosexual relationships. *Violence Against Women* 8: 1364–1389.

Dobash, R.E., and Dobash, R.P. (1979). *Violence Against Wives*. New York, NY: The Free Press.

Downey, J.P., and Stage, F.K. (1999). Hate crimes and violence on college and university campuses. *Journal of College Student Development* 40: 3–9.

Downing, C. (1993). *Gods in our Midst: Mythological Images of the Masculine: A Woman's View*. New Orleans, LA: Spring Journal Books.

Dubin, W.R. (1981). Evaluating and managing the violent patient. *Annals of Emergency Medicine* 10: 481–484.

Dutton, D.G., and Painter, S.L. (1981). Traumatic bonding: The development of emotional attachments in battered women and other relationships of intermittent abuse. *Victimology* 6: 139–155.

Dutton, M.A., and Goodman, L.A. (2005). Coercion in intimate partner violence: Toward a new conceptualization. *Sex Roles* 52: 743–756.

Elkins, J. (2017). Revisiting destruction in "The Use of An Object." *Psychoanalytic Quarterly* 86: 109–148.

Elliott, P. (1996). Shattering illusions: Same-sex domestic violence. *Journal of Gay and Lesbian Social Services* 8: 1–4.

Elshtain, J.B. (2002). ed. *Just War Theory (Readings in Social and Political Theory)*. New York: New York University Press.

Erdos, B., and Hughes, D. (2001). Emergency psychiatry: A review of assaults by patients against staff at psychiatric emergency centers. *Psychiatric Services* 52: 1175–1177.

Erickson, E.H. (1950). *Childhood and Society*. New York: W.W. Norton.

Erikson, E.H. (1956). The problem of ego identity. *Journal of the American Psychoanalytic Association* 4: 56–121.

Erikson, E.H. (1959). *Identity and the Life Cycle. Psychological Issues Monograph No. 1*. New York: International Universities Press.

Feldman, T.B., Holt, J., and Hellard, S. (1997). Violence in medical facilities: A review of 40 incidents. *Journal of the Kentucky Medical Association* 5: 183–189.

Fischer, N. (1971). An interracial analysis: Transference and countertransference significance. *Journal of the American Psychoanalytic Association* 19: 736–745.

Foust, D., and Rhee, K.J. (1993). The incidence of battery in an urban emergency department. *Annals of Emergency Medicine* 22: 583–585.

Freud, S. (1893). On the psychical mechanism of hysterical phenomena: A lecture. *Standard Edition* 3: 25–41.

Freud, S. (1895). Studies on hysteria (with Joseph Breuer). *Standard Edition* 2: 1–323.

Freud, S. (1912–1913). Totem and taboo. *Standard Edition* 13: 1–161.

Freud, S. (1921). Group psychology and the analysis of the ego. *Standard Edition* 18: 65–143.

Freud, S. (1925). Some psychical consequences of the anatomical distinction between the sexes. *Standard Edition* 19: 248–258.

Freud, S. (1927). The future of an illusion. *Standard Edition* 21: 5–56.

Freud, S. (1933). New introductory lectures on psycho-analysis, XXXIII: Femininity. *Standard Edition* 22: 112–135.

Freud, S. (1935). An autobiographical study. *Standard Edition* 20: 7–74.

Freud, S. (1939). An outline of psycho-analysis. *Standard Edition* 23: 141–207.

Friedman, M., Grawert, A.C., and Cullen, J. (2017). *Crime Trends: 1990–2016, Twenty Years*. New York: Brennan Center for Justice at New York University School of Law.

Frieze, I.H. (1979). Perception of battered wives. In: *New Approaches to Social Problems: Applications of Attribution Theory*, eds. I.H. Frieze, D. Bar-Tal and J.S. Carroll, pp. 79–108. San Francisco, CA: Jossey Bass.

Garnets, L., Herek, G.M., and Levy, B. (1990). Violence and victimization of lesbians and gay men: Mental health consequences. *Journal of Interpersonal Violence* 5: 366–383.

Geertz, C. (1993). *The Interpretation of Cultures: Selected Essays*. London: Fontana Press, pp. 87–125.

Gentile, K. (2013). Bearing the cultural in order to engage the process of witnessing. *Psychodynamic Psychology* 30: 456–470.

Ghent, E. (1990). Masochism, submission, surrender: Masochism as a perversion of surrender. *Contemporary Psychoanalysis* 26: 108–136.

Goldberg, E.L., Myers, W.A., and Zeifman, I. (1974). Some observations on three interracial analyses. *International Journal of Psycho-Analysis* 55: 495–500.

Gondolf, E., and Fisher, E.R. (1988). *Battered Women as Survivors: An Alternative to Treating Learned Helplessness*. Lexington, MA: Lexington Books.

Greenson, R. (1968). Disidentifying from the mother. *International Journal of Psychoanalysis* 49: 370–374.

Greenwood, G.L., Relf, M.V., Huang, B., Pollack, L.M., Canchola, M.S., and Cantania, J.A. (2002). Battering victimization among a probability-based sample of men who have sex with men. *American Journal of Public Health* 92: 1964–1969.

Haarer, J. (1934). *Die deutsche Mutter und ihr erstes Kind*. München: Lehmanns.

Haarer, J. (1937). Mutterschaft und Familienpflege imneuen Reich (Motherhood and Family Care in the New Reich). In: *Beiträge zur Volkslehr und Gemeinschaftspflege (Essays on Ethnology and Community Care)*. Munich, Germany: Herausgegeben von der Volksbildungs Kanzlei.

Haarer, J. (1943). *Mutter, Erzähl von Adolf Hitler (Mother, Tell me about Adolf Hitler.)* Munich, Germany: J.F. Lehmanns Verlag.

Hamberger, L.K., and Hastings, J.E. (1991). Personality correlates of men who batter and nonviolent men: Some continuities and discontinuities. *Journal of Family Violence* 6: 131–147.

Harle, V. (2000). *The Enemy with a Thousand Faces: The Tradition of the Other in Western Political Thought and History.* Westport, CT: Praeger.

Hartmann, H. (1939). *Ego Psychology and the Problem of Adaptation*, transl. D. Rapaport. New York, NY: International Universities Press, 1958.

Hedges, C. (2002). *War is a Force that Gives Us Meaning.* New York: Anchor Books.

Heintz, A.J., and Melendez, R.M. (2006). Intimate partner violence and HIV/STD risk among lesbian, gay, bisexual, and transgender individuals. *Journal of Interpersonal Violence* 21: 193–208.

Herek, G.M., Gillis, J.R., and Cogan, J.C. (2000). Psychological sequelae of hate-crime victimization among lesbian, gay, and bisexual adults. *Journal of Consulting and Clinical Psychology* 67: 945–961.

Herodotus (ca 440 BCE). (1987). *The History.* Chicago, IL: University of Chicago Press.

Hollander, N.C. (2010). Anti-Muslim prejudice and the psychic use of the ethnic other. *International Journal of Applied Psychoanalytic Studies* 7: 73–84.

Holmes, D.E. (1992). Race and transference in psychoanalysis and psychotherapy. *International Journal of Psycho-Analysis* 73: 1–11.

Holmes, D.E. (2016). Culturally imposed trauma: The sleeping dog has awakened. Will psychoanalysis take heed? *Psychoanalytic Dialogues* 26: 641–654.

Homer (circa 900 BC). (1999). *The Iliad.* Loeb Classical Library, Harvard University Press.

Horney, K. (1945). *Our Inner Conflicts.* New York: W.W. Norton.

Horney, K. (1950). *Neurosis and Human Growth.* New York: W.W. Norton.

Howell, W.N. (1997). Islamic revivalism: A cult phenomenon? *Mind and Human Interaction* 5: 97–103.

http://britannica.com/event/Enlightenment-European-history

http://en.wikipedia.org/wiki/Enlightenment

https://en.wikipedia.org/wiki/Two_Treatises_of_Government

https://www.britannica.com/biography/John-Locke

Iozzino, L., Ferrari, C., Large, M., Nielssen, O., and de Girolamo, G. (2015). Prevalence and risk factors of violence by psychiatric acute inpatients: a systematic review and meta-analysis. *PLoS One.* 2015 Jun 10;10(6):e0128536. doi: 10.1371/journal.pone.0128536. eCollection 2015.

Island, D., and Letellier, P. (1991). *Men Who Beat the Men Who Love Them: Battered Gay Men and Domestic Violence.* Binghamton, NY: Haworth.

Ito, H., Eisen, S., Sederer, L., Yamada, O., and Tachimoro, H. (2001). Factors affecting psychiatric nurses' intention to leave their current job. *Psychiatric Services* 52: 232–234.

James, W. (1902). *The Varieties of Religious Experience: A Study in Human Nature.* New York: The Library of America, 1987.

Jones, A. (1981). *Women Who Kill.* New York: Holt, Rinehart and Winston.

Jung, C.G. (1936). *WOTAN.* Zurich, Switzerland: Neue Schweizer Rundschau.

Kagan, J., and Herschkowitz, N. (2005). *A Young Mind in a Growing Child.* Mahwah, NJ: Lawrence Erlbaum Associates.

Kakar, S. (1996). *The Colors of Violence: Cultural Identities, Religion, and Conflict.* Chicago, IL: University of Chicago Press.

Katan, A. (1961). Some thoughts about the role of verbalization in early childhood. *The Psychoanalytic Study of the Child* 16: 184–188.

Kedourie, E. (1970). *The Chatham House Version: And Other Middle Eastern Studies.* London: Weidenfeld and Nicholson.

Kelly, L. (1987). The continuum of sexual violence. In: *Women, Violence and Social Control. Explorations in Sociology (British Sociological Association Conference Volume series)*, eds. J. Hanmer and M. Maynard, pp. 46–60. London: Palgrave Macmillan.

Kelly, L. (1989). *Surviving Sexual Violence.* Minneapolis, MN: University of Minnesota Press.

Kernberg, O.F. (1980). *Internal World and External Reality: Object Relations Theory Applied.* New York: Jason Aronson.

Kernberg, O. (1995). Hatred as a core affect of aggression. In: *The Birth of Hatred: Clinical, Developmental, Clinical, and Technical Aspects of Intense Aggression*, eds. S. Akhtar, S. Kramer and H. Parens, pp. 53–82. Northvale, NJ: Jason Aronson.

Kestenberg, J.S., and Brenner, I. (1996). *The Last Witness: The Child Survivor of the Holocaust.* Washington DC: American Psychiatric Press, Inc.

Khan, M. (1972). Dread of surrender to resourceless dependence in the analytic situation. *International Journal of Psycho-Analysis* 53: 225–230.

Klein, M. (1940). Mourning and its relation to manic depressive states. In: *Love, Guilt, and Reparation, and Other Works – 1921–1945*, pp. 344–369. New York: Free Press, 1975.

Knafo, D. (1999). Anti-semitism in the clinical setting: Transference and countertransference dimensions. *Journal of the American Psychoanalytic Association* 47: 35–63.

Kogan, I. (1995). *The Cry of Mute Children—A Psychoanalytic Perspective of the Second Generation of the Holocaust.* London: Free Association Books.

Krystal, H. (1968). *Massive Psychic Trauma.* New York: International Universities Press.

Kuriloff, E.A. (2014). *Contemporary Psychoanalysis and the Legacy of the Third Reich.* New York: Routledge.

Lanza, M.L. (1996). The multiple costs of patient assault. In: *Creating a Secure Workplace: Effective Policies and Practices in Health Care*, eds. W.R. Dubin, D.E. Futrell and J.R. Lion, pp. 25–39. Chicago, IL: American Hospital Publishing Inc.

Latane, B., and Darley, J.M. (1970). *The Unresponsive Bystander: Why Doesn't He Help?* Englewood Cliffs, NJ: Prentice Hall.

Layton, L. (2006). Racial identities, racial enactments, and normative unconscious processes. *Psychoanalytic Quarterly* 75: 237–269.

Leary, K. (1995). Interpreting in the dark: Race and ethnicity in psychoanalytic psychotherapy. *Psychoanalytic Psychology* 12: 127–140.

Leary, K. (1997a). Race in psychoanalytic space. *Gender and Psychoanalysis* 2: 157–172.

Leary, K. (1997b). Race, self-disclosure, and 'forbidden talk': Race, ethnicity in contemporary practice. *Psychoanalytic Quarterly* 66: 163–189.

Leary, K. (2000). Racial enactments in dynamic treatment. *Psychoanalytic Dialogues* 10: 639–653.

Leary, K. (2007). Racial insult and repair. *Psychoanalytic Dialogues* 17: 539–549.

Leidig, M J. (1992). The continuum of violence against women: Psychological and physical consequences. *Journal of American College Health* 40: 149–155.

Lenin, V.I. (1906). Guerilla warfare. In: *Lenin Collected Works* 11: 213–223. Moscow: Progress Publishers, 1965.

Letellier, P. (1996). Twin epidemics: Domestic violence and HIV infection among gay and bisexual men. In: *Violence in Gay and Lesbian Domestic Partnerships,* eds. C.M. Renzetti and C.H. Miley, pp. 69–82. Binghamton, NY: Harrington Park.

Levi, P. (1958). *Survival in Auschwitz.* Translated from *Se Questo e un Uomo* ("If this is a Man") by Stuart Wolf. New York: Touchstone Books, 1996.

Levin, J., and McDevitt, J. (1995). The research need to understand hate crime. *The Chronicle of Higher Education* 41: B1–B2.

Lewin, R.A., and Schulz, C. (1992). *Losing and Fusing: Borderline Transitional Object and Self Relations*. Northvale, NJ: Jason Aronson.

Lewis, B. (1990). The roots of Moslem rage. *The Atlantic Monthly*, September 20, pp. 47–60.

Littman A., and Flegenheimer, M. (2017). Neil Gorsuch confirmed by Senate as Supreme Court Justice. *The New York Times*, April 7, 2017.

Loewenberg, P. (1995). *Fantasy and Reality in History*. London: Oxford University Press.

Lucas, R. (2015). IS militants kidnap dozens of Christians in Syria. *NPR, Associated Press*, 12 noon, February 24, 2015.

Madden, D.J., Lion, J.R., and Penna, M.W. (1976). Assaults on psychiatrists by patients. *American Journal of Psychiatry* 133: 422–425.

Mahler, M.S., Bergman, A., and Pine, F. (1957). *The Psychological Birth of the Human Infant*. New York: Basic Books.

McDevitt, J.B. (1983). The emergence of hostile aggression and its defensive and adaptive modifications during the separation-individuation process. *Journal of the American Psychoanalytic Association* 31: 273–300.

McDevitt, J., Levin, J., and Bennett, S. (2002). Hate crime offenders: An expanded typology. *Journal of Social Issues* 58: 303–317.

McEllistrem, J. (2004). Affective and predatory violence: A bimodal classification system of human aggression and violence. *Aggression and Violent Behavior* 10: 1–30.

McHugh, M.C., and Frieze, I.H. (2006). Intimate partner violence: New directions. *Annals of the New York Academy of the Sciences* 1087: 121–141.

McMahon, S. (2010). Rape myth beliefs and bystander attitudes among incoming college students. *Journal of American College Health* 59: 3–11.

McMahon, S., and Banyard, V.L. (2012). When can I help? A conceptual framework for the prevention of sexual violence through bystander intervention. *Trauma, Violence, and Abuse* 13: 3–14.

Melroy, J.R., Hempel, A.G., Gray, B.T., Mohandie, K., Shiva, A., and Richards, T.C. (2004). A comparative analysis of North American adolescent and adult mass murderers. *Behavioral Sciences and the Law* 22: 291–309.

Morrison, E.F. (1993). Toward a better understanding of violence in psychiatric settings: Debunking the myths. *Archives of Psychiatric Nursing* 7: 328–335.

Morrison, E.F. (1994). The evolution of a concept: Aggression and violence in psychiatric settings. *Archives of Psychiatric Medicine* 8: 245–253.

Morrison, J., Lantos, J.D., and Levinson, W. (1998). Aggression and violence directed toward physicians. *Journal of General Internal Medicine* 13: 556–561.

My Name Is Khan (2010). Directed by K. Johar, produced by Dharma Productions.

Nolan, P., Dallender, J., Soares, J., Thomsen, S., Arnetz, B. (1999). Violence in mental health care: The experiences of mental health nurses and psychiatrists. *Journal of Advanced Nursing* 30: 934–941.

Novick J., and Novick, K.K. (2005). Soul blindness: A child must be seen to be heard. In: *Divorce and Custody: Contemporary Developmental Psychoanalytic Perspectives*, eds. L. Gunsberg and P. Hymowitz, pp. 81–90. Washington, DC: American Psychological Association Books.

Novick, J., and Novick, K.K. (2016). *Freedom to Choose: Two Systems of Self-Regulation*. New York: IPBooks.

Novick, K.K., and Novick, J. (2010). *Emotional Muscle: Strong Parents, Strong Children*. Bloomington, IN: XLibris Publishing.

Novick, K.K., and Novick, J. (2014). Psychoanalysis and child rearing. *Psychoanalytic Inquiry* 34: 440–451.

Oberndorf, C.P. (1954). Selectivity and option for psychiatry. *American Journal of Psychiatry* 110: 754–758.

Ogden, T. (2016). Destruction reconceived: On Winnicott's 'The Use of an Object and Relating through Identifications.' *International Journal of Psychoanalysis* 97: 1243–1262.

Olofsson, B., and Jacobsson, L. (2001). A plea for respect: Involuntarily hospitalized psychiatric patients' narratives about being subjected to coercion. *Journal of Psychiatric and Mental Health Nursing* 8: 357–366.

Olsson, P.A. (2008). Ideology and aggression: Osama bin Laden. In: *The Crescent and the Couch: Cross-Currents Between Islam and Psychoanalysis*, ed. S. Akhtar, pp. 103–119. Lanham, MD: Jason Aronson.

Ornstein, A. (2004). *My Mother's Eyes—Holocaust Memories of a Young Girl*. Cincinnati, OH: Emmis Press.

Osborne, R. (1995). The continuum of violence against women in Canadian universities: Toward a new understanding of the chilly campus climate. *Women's Studies International Forum* 18: 637–646.

Owen, C., Tarantello, C., and Jones, M. (1998). Violence and aggression in psychiatric units. *Psychiatric Services* 49: 1452–1457.

Pagelow, M. (1981). *Woman-Battering*. Beverly Hills, CA: Sage.

Parens, H. (1979). *The Development of Aggression in Early Childhood*. Lanham, MD: Jason Aronson/Rowman and Littlefield Publishers, 2008.

Parens, H. (1987). Cruelty begins at home. *Child Abuse and Neglect* 11: 331–338.

Parens, H. (2004). *Renewal of Life—Healing from the Holocaust.* Rockville, MD: Schreiber Publishing, 2014.

Parens, H. (2007). Toward understanding prejudice—benign and malignant. In: *The Future of Prejudice: Psychoanalysis and the Prevention of Prejudice,* eds. H. Parens, A. Mahfouz, S. Twemlow and D. Scharff, pp. 21–36. Lanham, MD: Rowman and Littlefield Publishers.

Parens, H. (2011). *Handling Children's Aggression Constructively—Toward Taming Human Destructiveness.* Lanham, MD: Jason Aronson/Rowman and Littlefield Publishers, Inc.

Parens, H. (2012). *Taming Aggression in Your Child: How to Avoid Raising Bullies, Delinquents and Other Trouble-Makers.* Lanham, MD: Jason Aronson/Rowman and Littlefield Publishers.

Parens, H. (2014). *War is Not Inevitable—On the Psychology of War and Aggression.* Lanham, MD: Lexington Books.

Parens, H. (2016). The changing morphology of parenthood—its implications for separation-individuation theory. In: *The New Motherhoods: Patterns of Early Child Care in Contemporary Culture,* ed. S. Akhtar, pp. 15–40. Lanham, MD: Jason Aronson/Rowman and Littlefield Publishers.

Parens, H., Scattergood, E., Duff, A., and Singletary, W. (1995). *Parenting for Emotional Growth:* (a) *The Textbook;* and (b) *A Curriculum for Students in Grades K Thru 12.* Philadelphia: Parenting for Emotional Growth, Inc. © TXu 680–613. Available free of charge at http://jdc.jefferson.edu/parentingemotionalgrowth

Parsons, T. (1967). *The Structure of Social Action,* Volumes 1 and 2. New York: Free Press.

Pence, E., and Paymar, M. (1993). *Education Groups for Men Who Batter: The Duluth Model.* New York: Springer.

Prager, J. (2015). A review of 'Enemies on the Couch by Vamik Volkan.' *The International Journal of Psychoanalysis* 96: 503–506.

Privitera, M., Weisman, R., Cerulli, C., and Groman, A. (2005). Violence toward mental health staff and safety in the work environment. *Occupational Medicine* 55: 480–486.

Rashid, A. (2000). *Taliban: Islam, Oil and the New Great Game in Central Asia.* London: I.B. Tauris.

Renzetti, C.M. (1989). Building a second closet: Third-party responses to victims of lesbian partner abuse. *Family Relations* 38: 157–163.

Renzetti, C.M. (1992). *Violent Betrayal: Partner Abuse in Lesbian Relationships.* Newbury Park, CA: Sage.

Rice, M.M., and Moore, G.P. (1991). Management of the violent patient: Therapeutic and legal considerations. *Emergency Medicine Clinics of North America* 9: 13–30.

Ridington, J. (1978). The transition process: A feminist environment as reconstructive milieu. *Victimology* 3: 563–575.

Roche, M., Diers, D., Duffield, C., and Catling-Paull, C. (2009). Violence toward nurses, the work environment and patient outcomes. *Journal of Nursing Scholarship* 42: 12–22.

Ross, J., Quayle, E., Newman, E., and Tansey, L. (2013). The impact of psychological therapies on violent behaviour in clinical and forensic settings: A systematic review. *Aggression and Violent Behavior* 18: 761–773.

Rueve, M., and Welton, R. (2008). Violence and mental illness. *Psychiatry* 5: 34–48.

Rutschky, K., ed. (2001). *Schwarze Pädagogik. Quellen zur Naturgeschichte der bürgerlichen Erziehung,* 8th ed. Munich: Ullstein-Bücher, Allgemeine Reihe.

Sadler, A.G., Booth, B.M., Nielson, D., and Doebbeling, B.N. (2000). Health-related consequences of physical and sexual violence: Women in the military. *Obstetrics and Gynecology* 96: 473–480.

Sanday, P.R. (2007). *Fraternity Gang Rape*, 2nd ed. New York: New York University Press.

Sanguineti, V. (2007). *A Rosetta Stone to the Human Mind.* New York: Springer.

Schachter, J.S., and Butts, H.F. (1968). Transference and countertransference in interracial analyses. *Journal of the American Psychoanalytic Association* 16: 792–780.

Schwartz, M.D., and Dekeseredy, W.S. (1997). *Sexual Assault on the College Campus: The Role of Male Peer Support.* Thousand Oaks, CA: SAGE.

Seelau, S.M., and Seelau, E.P. (2005). Gender-role stereotypes and perceptions of heterosexual, gay and lesbian domestic violence. *Journal of Family Violence* 20: 363–371.

Sheridan, M., Henrion, R., Robinson, L., and Baxter, V. (1990). Precipitants of violence in a psychiatric inpatient setting. *Hospital and Community Psychiatry* 41: 776–780.

Slavin, J. (2010). Becoming an individual: Technically subversive thoughts on the role of the analyst's influence. *Psychoanalytic Dialogues* 20: 308–324.

Sofield, L., and Salmound, S. (2003). Workplace violence: A focus on verbal abuse and intent to leave the organization. *Orthopaedic Nursing* 22: 274–283.

Speckhard, A., and Yayla, A.S. (2015). Eyewitness accounts from recent defectors from Islamic State: Why they joined, what they saw, why they quit. *Perspectives on Terrorism* 9: 95–116.

Spitz, R. (1965). *The First Year of Life.* New York: International Universities Press.

Stahly, G.B. (1996). Battered women: Why don't they just leave? In: *Lectures on the Psychology of Women*, eds. J.C. Chrisler, C. Golden and P.D. Rozee, pp. 289–308. New York: McGraw-Hill.

Stewart, D.E., and Vigod, S.N. (2017). Mental health aspects of intimate partner violence. *Psychiatric Clinics of North America* 40: 321–334.

Stout, K.D. (1991). A continuum of male controls and violence against women: A teaching model. *Journal of Social Work* 27: 305–320.

Stout, K.D., and McPhail, B. (1998). *Confronting Sexism and Violence Against Women: A Challenge for Social Work.* New York: Longman.

Suarez, E., and Gadalla, T.M. (2010). Stop blaming the victim: A meta-analysis on rape myths. *Journal of Interpersonal Violence* 25: 2010–2035.

Sucharov, M. (2013). Politics, race, and class in the analytic space: The healing power of therapeutic advocacy. *International Journal of Psychoanalytic Self Psychology* 8: 29–45.

Sugarman, D., and Frankel, S.I. (1996). Patriarchal ideology and wife-assault: A meta-analytic review. *Journal of Family Violence* 11: 13–40.

Suistola, J., and Volkan, V.D. (2017). *Gods Do Negotiate: International Terror and Religious Knives*. Durham, NC: Pitchstone.

Sullaway, M. (2004). Psychological perspectives on hate crime. *Psychology, Public Policy, and Law* 10: 250–292.

Sullivan, C.M., Basta, J., Tan, C., and Davidson, II, W.S. (1992). After the crisis: A needs assessment of women leaving a domestic violence shelter. *Violence and Victims* 7: 267–275.

Swanson, J. (2008). Preventing the unpredicted: Managing violence risk in mental health care. *Psychiatric Services* 59: 191–193.

Thomson, J.A. [with C. Aukofer] (2011). *Why We Believe in God(s): A Concise Guide to the Science of Faith*. Charlottesville, VA: Pitchstone.

Ticho, G. (1971). Cultural aspects of transference and countertransference. *Bulletin of the Menninger Clinic* 35: 313–326.

Time (1999). December 20, 1999, p. 44.

Tolman, R.M., and Bennett, L.W. (1990). A review of quantitative research on men who batter. *Journal of Interpersonal Violence* 5: 87–118.

Turell, S.T. (2000). A descriptive analysis of same-sex relationship violence for a diverse sample. *Journal of Family Violence* 15: 281–293.

Twemlow, S. (2000). Psychoanalytic thinking applied to social issues: A vision of the future. *Journal of Applied Psychoanalytic Studies* 2: 209–218.

Volkan, V.D. (1976). *Primitive Internalized Object Relations*. New York, NY: International Universities Press.

Volkan, V.D. (1988). *The Need to Have Enemies and Allies: From Clinical Practice to International Relationships*. Northvale, NJ: Jason Aronson.

Volkan, V.D. (1991). On chosen trauma. *Mind and Human Interaction* 4: 3–19.

Volkan, V.D. (1996). Bosnia-Herzegovina: Ancient fuel of a modern inferno. *Mind and Human Interaction* 7: 110–127.

Volkan, V.D. (1997). *Bloodlines: From Ethnic Pride to Ethnic Terrorism*. New York: Farrar, Straus and Giroux.

Volkan, V.D. (2004). *Blind Trust: Large Groups and Their Leaders in Times of Crises and Terror*. Charlottesville, VA: Pitchstone.

Volkan, V.D. (2006). *Killing in the Name of Identity: A Study of Bloody Conflicts*. Charlottesville, VA: Pitchstone.

Volkan, V.D. (2010). A discussion: Psychoanalytic considerations on large-group psychology. *Fall Newsletter of the American College of Psychoanalysts* 44: 5–7.

Volkan, V.D. (2013). *Enemies on the Couch: A Psychopolitical Journey through War and Peace*. Durham, NC: Pitchstone.

Volkan, V.D. (2014). *Psychoanalysis, International Relations, and Diplomacy: A Sourcebook on Large-Group Psychology*. London: Karnac.

Volkan, V.D. (2017). Gods do not negotiate: A psychohistorical look at terrorism. In: *Before and After Violence: Developmental, Clinical, and Social Aspects*, ed. S. Akhtar. Lanham, MD: Jason Aronson (in press).

Volkan, V.D. (2017). *Immigrants and Refugees: Trauma, Perennial Mourning, and Border Psychology*. London: Karnac.

Volkan, V.D., Ast, G., and Greer, W. (2002). *The Third Reich in the Unconscious: Transgenerational Transmissions and its Consequences*. New York: Brunner-Routledge.

Waelder, R. (1936). The principle of multiple function: Observations on multiple determination. *Psychoanalytic Quarterly* 41: 283–290.

Waldner-Haugrud, L., Gratch, L., and Magruder, B. (1997). Victimization and perpetration rates of violence in gay and lesbian relationships: Gender issues explored. *Violence and Victims* 12: 173–182.

Walker, L.E. (1979). *The Battered Woman*. New York: Harper and Row.

Walker, L.E. (1983). The battered woman syndrome study. In: *The Dark Side of Families: Current Family Violence Research*, eds. D. Finkelhor, R.J. Gelles, G.T. Hotalling and M.A. Straus, pp. 31–47. Beverly Hills, CA: Sage.

Walker, L.E. (1984). *The Battered Woman Syndrome*. New York: Springer.

Wallerstein, R.S. (1983). Self psychology and 'classical' psychoanalytic psychology: The nature of their relationship. In: *The Future of Psychoanalysis*, ed. A. Goldberg, pp. 19–63. New York: International Universities Press.

Walsh, F. (1996). Partner abuse. In: *Pink Therapy: A Guide for Counsellors and Therapists Working with Lesbian, Gay, and Bisexual Clients*, eds. D. Davies and C. Neal, pp. 188–198. Buckingham, UK: Open University Press.

Welsh, E., Bader, S., and Evans, S.E. (2013). Situational variables related to aggression in institutional settings. *Aggression and Violent Behaviour* 18: 792–796.

Whitman, R.M., Armao B.B., and Dent, O.B. (1976). Assault on the therapist. *American Journal of Psychiatry* 133: 426–429.

Winnicott, D.W. (1947). Hate in the countertransference. In: *Through Paediatrics to Psychoanalysis: Collected Papers*, pp. 194–203. New York, NY: Brunner/Mazel, 1992.

Winnicott, D.W. (1953). Transitional objects and transitional phenomena—a study of the first not-me possession. *International Journal of Psychoanalysis* 34: 89–97.

Winnicott, D.W. (1960). The theory of parent-infant relationship. In: *The Maturational Processes and the Facilitating Environment*, pp. 37–55. New York: International Universities Press, 1965.

Winnicott, D.W. (1969). The use of an object. *International Journal of Psychoanalysis* 50: 711–716.

Winnicott, D.W. (1971). *Playing and Reality*. London: Penguin Books.

Winnicott, D.W. (1971). The use of an object and relating through identifications. In: *Playing and Reality*, pp. 86–94. London: Penguin Books.

Yang, L.-Q., Spector, P.E., Chang, C.-H., Gallant-Roman, M., and Powell, J. (2012). Psychosocial precursors and physical consequences of workplace violence towards nurses: A longitudinal examination with naturally occurring groups in hospital settings. *International Journal of Nursing Studies* 49: 1091–1102.

Zolotor, A.J., Denham, A.C., and Weil, A. (2009). Intimate partner violence. *Primary Care: Clinics in Office Practice* 36: 167–179.

Index

About the Contributors

Aisha Abbasi, MD, is training and supervising analyst and immediate past president of the Michigan Psychoanalytic Institute. She maintains a practice of psychotherapy and psychoanalysis in West Bloomfield, Michigan.

Salman Akhtar, MD, is professor of psychiatry at Jefferson Medical College and training and supervising analyst at the Psychoanalytic Center of Philadelphia.

Suzanne Benser, MD, is faculty member, psychoanalytic center of Philadelphia, Philadelphia, Pennsylvania. She maintains a practice of psychotherapy and psychoanalysis in Bala Cynwyd, Pennsylvania.

Shawn Blue, PhD, is assistant professor, Sidney Kimmel Medical College; psychologist, Student Personal Counseling Center, Department of Psychiatry and Human Behavior, Thomas Jefferson University, Philadelphia, Pennsylvania.

Kerry Kelly Novick, AB, BA, is training and supervising analyst, international psychoanalytic association and faculty member, Michigan Psychoanalytic Institute. She maintains a private practice of psychotherapy and psychoanalysis in Ann Arbor, Michigan.

Henri Parens, MD, professor of psychiatry, Thomas Jefferson University, and training & supervising analyst (adult and child), Psychoanalytic Center of Philadelphia. He maintains a practice of psychotherapy and psychoanalysis in Bala Cynwyd, Pennsylvania.

Vincenzo Sanguineti, MD, is associate professor at Jefferson Medical College in Philadelphia. He is presently in private practice in Philadelphia, Pennsylvania.

Ann Smolen, PhD, is supervising and training analyst in child, adolescent, and adult psychoanalysis at the Psychoanalytic Center of Philadelphia. She maintains a private practice in child, adolescent, and adult psychotherapy and psychoanalysis in Ardmore, Pennsylvania.

Vamık Volkan, MD, DFLAPA, FACPsa, is emeritus professor of Psychiatry at the University of Virginia, Charlottesville, and an emeritus training and supervising analyst at the Washington Psychoanalytic Institute, Washington, DC.